The Holy Spirit,
Lord and Giver of Life

Prepared by
The Theological-Historical Commission
for the Great Jubilee of the Year 2000

Translated from the Italian by
Agostino Bono

A Crossroad Herder Book
The Crossroad Publishing Company
New York

This printing: 1998

The Crossroad Publishing Company
370 Lexington Avenue, New York, NY 10017

Original edition: *Del tuo Spirito, è piena la terra*
Copyright © 1997 by Edizioni San Paolo (Milan)

English translation Copyright © 1997
by The Crossroad Publishing Company

Printed in the United States of America

Library of Congress Cataloging-in-Publication Data

Del tuo spirito, e piena la terra. English
    The Holy Spirit, Lord and giver of life / prepared by the
Theological-Historical Commission for the Great Jubilee of the Year
2000 ; translated from the Italian by Agostino Bono.
      p. cm.
    Includes bibliographical references.
    ISBN 0-8245-1704-0
    1. Holy Spirit. 2. Catholic Church – Doctrines.   I. Theological-
Historical Commission for the Great Jubilee of the Year 2000.
BT121.2.D37513   1997
231′.3 – dc21   97-18445
                                          CIP

Contents

Abbreviations 7

Introduction 11

1. The Mediation of the Holy Spirit in the Trinity
   and in Salvation 15
   God "Is" Trinity   15
   Each Divine Person Possesses Something Personal That
        Distinguishes Him   17
   "In the Holy Spirit"   21
   Conclusion   28

2. The Spirit and Creation 30
   God the Father Creates through the Word
        in the Power of the Spirit   31
   The Salvific Meaning of Creation in the Spirit   33
   Creation Is "Good," Existing in the Spirit
        and for the Spirit   35
   Conclusion   38

3. The Spirit and Humanity 41
   Humanity Is "Spiritual" by the Work of the Spirit
        and in the Spirit   42
   The Spirit Imprints the Image of God in Humanity   44
   Conclusion   48

4. The Holy Spirit and Christ 51
   Jesus Possesses the Spirit   51
   The Crucified-Resurrected One Bestows the Spirit   54
   Conclusion   58

5. The Holy Spirit and the Church 60

The Church Is One in Virtue of the Spirit   61
The Church Is Holy in Virtue of the Sanctifying Spirit   64
The Church Is Catholic in the Fullness of the Spirit   67
The Church Is Apostolic through the Perpetual Sending
   of the Spirit   69
The Church Spreads by Evangelizing in the Spirit   72
Conclusion   77

6. Mary and the Spirit 80

Mary, Docile Resting Place of the Spirit   80
Mary in Virtue of the Spirit Becomes Mother of God   83
In the Spirit Mary Continues to Be the Mother
   of the Body of Christ   86
Conclusion   88

7. The Holy Spirit in the Liturgy 91

The Holy Spirit, Soul of the Liturgy   92
The Presence and Action of the Spirit in the Sacraments   96
Conclusion   115

8. The Spirit in the Life of Christians 117

The Spirit Makes Us Participators in the Divine Life   118
The Spirit Prepares Us to Welcome the Divine Life with Faith   119
In the Spirit We Become Children of God in the Son   122
Conclusion   141

9. The Bride and the Spirit Say: Come 147

The Spirit, Guarantee of the Resurrection   148
Expectation and Judgment in the Spirit   149
The Ultimate Reality Begins Now in the Spirit   150
In Watchful Expectation   151
Crossing the Threshold of Hope   153

Abbreviations

CCC   *Catechism of the Catholic Church* (1992)

ChL   *Christifideles Laici,* post-synodal apostolic exhortation of Pope John Paul II on the vocation and mission of the laity (December 30, 1988)

CT   *Catechesis Tradendae,* post-synodal apostolic exhortation of Pope John Paul II on catechesis (October 8, 1979)

DeV   *Dominum et Vivificantem,* encyclical letter of Pope John Paul II on the Holy Spirit (May 18, 1986)

DV   *Dei Verbum,* Dogmatic Constitution on Divine Revelation of the Second Vatican Council (November 18, 1965)

EH   *The Holy Spirit, Guarantee of Eschatological Hope and Source of Final Perseverance,* general audience speech of July 3, 1991, of Pope John Paul II, 14, no. 2

DS   *Enchiridion Symbolorum, Definitionum et Declarationum de Rebus Fidei et Morum,* ed. H. Denzinger, A. Schönmetzer (1965)

EN   *Evangelii Nuntiandi,* apostolic exhortation of Paul VI on evangelization (December 18, 1974)

EV   *Evangelium Vitae,* encyclical letter of Pope John Paul II on the value of human life (March 25, 1995)

GS   *Gaudium et Spes*, Pastoral Constitution on the Church in the Modern World of the Second Vatican Council (December 7, 1965)

LG   *Lumen Gentium*, Dogmatic Constitution on the Church of the Second Vatican Council (November 21, 1964)

MC   *Marialis Cultus*, apostolic exhortation of Pope Paul VI on Marian devotion (February 2, 1974)

OL   *Orientale Lumen*, apostolic letter of Pope John Paul II for the one hundredth anniversary of *Orientalium Dignitas* of Pope Leo XIII (May 2, 1995)

PO   *Presbyterorum Ordinis*, Decree on the Ministry and Life of Priests of the Second Vatican Council (December 7, 1965)

RM   *Redemptoris Missio*, encyclical letter of Pope John Paul II on missionary activity (December 7, 1990)

RMa   *Redemptoris Mater*, encyclical letter of Pope John Paul II on the Blessed Virgin Mary (March 25, 1987)

SC   *Sacrosanctum Concilium*, Constitution on the Liturgy of the Second Vatican Council (December 4, 1963)

TMA   *Tertio Millennio Adveniente*, apostolic letter of Pope John Paul II on the Great Jubilee of the year 2000 (November 10, 1994)

UR   *Unitatis Redintegratio*, Decree on Ecumenism of the Second Vatican Council (November 21, 1997)

UUS	*Ut Unum Sint,* encyclical letter of Pope John Paul II on ecumenism (May 25, 1995)
VC	*Vita Consecrata,* post-synodal apostolic exhortation of Pope John Paul II on religious life (March 25, 1996)
WA	*Martin Luthers Werke, Kritische Gesamtausgabe,* Weimar, 1883–

Introduction

John Paul II writes in reference to the preparations for the Jubilee year: "The year 1998, the second year of the preparatory phase, will be dedicated in a particular way to the Holy Spirit and to his sanctifying presence within the community of Christ's disciples" (*TMA*, 44). A year dedicated to the Holy Spirit seems absolutely necessary because, as the pontiff affirms, "The Church cannot prepare for the Jubilee in any other way than in the Holy Spirit" (*DeV*, 51). Beyond its christological connotation, the Great Jubilee "has a pneumatological aspect, since the mystery of the Incarnation was accomplished 'by the power of the Holy Spirit'" (*DeV*, 50). For this reason, "The primary tasks of the preparation for the Jubilee thus include a renewed appreciation of the presence and activity of the Spirit, who acts within the Church both in the sacraments, especially in Confirmation, and in the variety of charisms, roles, and ministries which he inspires for the good of the Church" (*TMA*, 45).

The current magisterium wishes to awaken "an increased sensitivity to all that the Spirit is saying to the Church and the Churches (cf. Rev. 2:7), as well as to individuals through charisms meant to serve the whole community. The purpose is to emphasize what the Spirit is suggesting to the different communities, from the smallest ones, such as the family, to the largest ones, such as nations and international organizations, taking into account cultures, societies, and sound traditions. Despite appearances, humanity continues to await the revelation of the children of God and lives by this hope, like a mother in labor, to use the image employed so powerfully by St. Paul in his letter to the Romans (see 8:19–22)" (*TMA*, 23).

This book offers an outline for reflection and better understanding of the teaching of the Holy Father. It is not intended to present a complete doctrine on the Holy Spirit. These pages are designed to be an instrument for meditation and, at the same time, an aid to religious instruction. To speak of the Holy Spirit is not easy. While the terms "Father" and "Son" applied to the first two persons of the Holy Trinity recall something "personal" and very familiar, the word "Spirit" alludes above all to biblical language, to "breath" and "wind."

As you will see in these pages, the Holy Spirit unveils the profundity of God, but his nature remains hidden. He reveals, yet remains in the shadows; he makes the Word concrete, but remains absolutely otherworldly. He turns the plan of God into history, but does not himself become history; he makes possible the incarnation of the Word but remains "Lord" in the absolute. He is in the very heart of every creature and gives life to every living thing, but remains "Spirit." His nature is so hidden that we can speak of him only indirectly, based on his actions and in the measure by which we experience him in his effects. Indeed, we can say that it is impossible to speak of the Holy Spirit except in the Holy Spirit himself. Otherwise, we run the risk of considering him as a simple "force" of God. He is a "person" distinct from the Father and the Son.

Because of this, rather than becoming preoccupied with saying "who" the Holy Spirit is, these pages will explain "what he does for us." We will attempt to explain the central themes of Christian doctrine starting with the experience of the Holy Spirit, a "discussion in virtue of the Holy Spirit." In presenting the mystery of the third divine person, we will go beyond recourse to biblical revelation and the documents of the magisterium. We will keep at hand the teachings of the Fathers of the Church who, having a unique and unsurpassed experience of the Holy Spirit, spoke of him in an unequaled way. Within this framework of reflection, the Fathers of the Eastern tradition are emphasized, while the Latin ones are not neglected; this is because the Greek Fathers needed to concern themselves with the Holy Spirit with greater frequency. This is also an "ecumenical" choice. We wanted to explain the doctrine of the Holy Spirit while walking in the footsteps of our Christian brothers and sisters of the East with the aim of raising a hymn to the Holy Spirit in the unison of East and West.

This text, therefore, hopes to be an instrument for reflection and prayer, so that the gift of the Holy Spirit might penetrate the life of every Christian. According to the word of Jesus, if a father on earth fulfills the prayers of his own sons, "how much more will the heavenly Father give the Holy Spirit to those who ask him?" (Luke 11:13). Praying for the gift of the Holy Spirit is so important that a variation of the Our Father exists, used by many Fathers of the Church. In place of the invocation "Thy kingdom come," it reads "Thy Spirit descend upon us and purify us" (see Gregory of Nyssa, *Homily on the Lord's Prayer*, III, 6). From this perspective we can then understand the words of a Russian saint of the last century, Seraphim of Sarov (d. 1833): "Prayer, fastings, vigils, and all other Christian practices...do not constitute the aim of our Christian life: they are but the indispensable means of attaining that aim. For the true aim of Christian life is the acquisition of the Holy Spirit of God."

The Great Jubilee will fulfill its function only if it becomes totally saturated with the presence and action of the Holy Spirit. "The year of grace" has no other goal except to create more favorable conditions for the Church and the body of Christ so that the Holy Spirit once again might renew and purify, reenacting during the time of the Jubilee that work of

Chapter 1

The Mediation of the Holy Spirit in the Trinity and in Salvation

Christian revelation never speaks of an impersonal God, of a force that threatens or inspires terror. It reveals a marvelous and exciting divine reality, who becomes personally involved. The God manifested by Jesus Christ is a personal God and the communion of three persons; this means the essence of God is *communion* (*koinonia*), that is, the Trinity.

God "Is" Trinity

The intimate, eternal life which constitutes God is his essence in communion. The unique and true God revealed by Jesus Christ is essentially and absolutely different from the god of any other religion. This affirmation is fundamental: everything stands firm or collapses in the measure to which the reality of God is or is not Trinity.

But what does it mean that God is Trinity? Might not this make us suspicious of mistaking or misunderstanding the oneness of God? Understanding the sense and significance of the trinitarian revelation of God the Father, the Son, and the Holy Spirit is possible only by referring to the message of the New Testament. The nucleus of faith in the early Christian community focused on Christ and his unique relationship to God and to salvation history. But it is just as evident that the absolutely singular mystery of Christ brings us back to the very essence of God, defining its very divinity. "Jesus revealed that God is Father in an unheard of sense:

he is Father not only in being Creator; he is eternally Father by his relationship to his only Son who, reciprocally, is Son only in relation to his Father" (CCC, 240). In other words, the Christian "good news" is the Gospel of the Trinity, and the divinity of God cannot be thought of, believed in, or professed except as the divinity of the Father, the Son, and the Holy Spirit. This is the ineffable mystery of God: if "God is Trinity," "the Trinity is the one and only God" (St. Augustine, *On the Trinity*, 7, 6, 12; 1, 6, 1).

From this perspective, we understand that at the basis of the triune essence of God is Easter as the culmination of the historical event that is Jesus Christ. In the gratuitous gift of himself, Jesus, the Son, expresses total obedience and openness to the will of the Father, in other words to the program of love which manifests the ultimate meaning of salvation. In this, the mystery of the cross (*theologia crucis*) takes on a paradigmatic value, above all because it reveals the paternity of God. In handing his Son over to death, God is seen not as an impassive God indifferent to human beings, but as the God of goodness and love whose infinity is in his love for each of us. It is a "paradoxical mystery of love: in Christ there suffers a God who has been rejected by his own creature" (*DeV*, 41). At the same time, Jesus in death entrusts himself to the Spirit (see John 19:30), in a faithful and filial abandonment, awaiting that reconciliation which will become full and definitive in the resurrection. "But now in Christ Jesus you who once were far off have been brought near by the blood of Christ...for through him both of us have access in one Spirit to the Father" (Eph. 2:13, 18).

The paschal event, therefore, in the paradox of the Crucified and Risen One, reveals the triune history of God in which communion and distinctiveness express the "truth" that is God (cf. CCC, 214–15), marked by a unique and unimaginable love. "In truth, to see the Trinity is to see love" (St. Augustine, *On the Trinity*, 8, 8, 12). This is the economy of salvation (cf. *CCC*, 236) in which the ultimate meaning of reality is safeguarded: if the essence of God is *communion* (*koinonia*), then all human beings, as creatures of God-Communion, will be called to communion with their Creator and with the rest of humanity. The God of Christian revelation "is one, but not solitary" (*Fides Damasi*, DS, 71). The Creed professes one God who in his essence *is* Father, Son, and Holy Spirit. This is our God: he is the mystery of love because he is the communion of three persons. This makes him a mystery of life without end.

If we consider that according to revelation "God is love" (1 John 4:16), we can understand the affirmation that the essence of God is Trinity-Communion. This expression means that God is God precisely because from all eternity the Father freely generates in love the Son and, with the Son, breathes forth the Holy Spirit.

This sets the framework for the theology of the first ecumenical councils and the theology of the Fathers of the Church. This theology is a profession of the trinitarian faith, from which comes the expression of Gregory of Nazianzus (d. ca. 390): "When I say 'God,' I mean the Father, the Son, and the Holy Spirit" (*Orations*, XLV, 4). This expression became absolutely normative for Christian "orthodoxy."

Each Divine Person Possesses Something Personal That Distinguishes Him

We believe in one God but his intimate life is so rich that it is formed by three persons distinct among themselves. Take seriously what is professed in the Creed: faith in one God in three equal but distinct persons means seeing in every divine person, in the light of revelation, that which is specific to him and distinguishes him from the others. In theological-ecclesial tradition the term "person" marks an important moment in the understanding of the incomprehensible mystery of God. As Scripture shows God manifesting himself in constant dialogue with humanity, the reflection of the Church underscores that God is a person because he is a Being in dialogue and in relationships. "The Church uses (1) the term 'substance' (rendered also at times by 'essence' or 'nature') to designate the divine being in its unity, (2) the term 'person' or 'hypostasis' to designate the Father, Son, and Holy Spirit in the real distinction among them, and (3) the term 'relation' to designate the fact that their distinction lies in the relationship of each to the others" (*CCC*, 252). The three divine persons, therefore, are one divinity formed of pure relationships, without any juxtapositions. In this sense, the being of the Father is the *beginning* of everything, the essence of the second person is *filial*, that is, the fact of being the Son, while the specific aspect of the third person is to be "spirated" (or draw his very origin) from the Father through the Son.

Regarding the eternal origin of the Holy Spirit, toward the end of the eighth century in the West there was added to the Nicene-Constantinople Creed the "Filioque" formula: "proceeds from the Father and the Son." Prior to that the Creed simply said "proceeds from the Father." To tell the truth, the formula "and the Son" was in use in the fifth century in the West in the creeds of some local Churches. It was officially introduced in the creed of the Church of Rome around 1013, after foreign pressure on Pope Benedict VIII by the emperor Henry II. For some time, this addition with the resulting doctrine of the proceeding of the Holy Spirit *from the Father and the Son* has been a serious point of disagreement for the Orthodox Churches.

In reality, these are two complementary methods of professing the same mystery. The *Catechism of the Catholic*

Church affirms: "At the outset the Eastern tradition expresses the Father's character as the first origin of the Spirit. By confessing the Spirit as he 'who proceeds from the Father,' it affirms that he comes *from* the Father *through* the Son. The Western tradition expresses first the consubstantial communion between Father and Son by saying that the Spirit proceeds from the Father and the Son (*filioque*).... This legitimate complementarity, provided it does not become rigid, does not affect the identity of faith in the reality of the same mystery confessed" (CCC, 248).

The above consideration concerns God "in himself." But in the history of salvation the Trinity also manifests itself as "the mystery of communion," so as to say "the union of the entire and royal Trinity ... with the whole human spirit" (Gregory of Nazianzus, *Orations*, 16, 9; cf. CCC, 2565). Although, as St. Augustine (d. 430) affirms, "the operations of the Trinity are inseparable" (*Sermons*, 71, 16), this does not mean that they are also indistinct. Every divine person, by the very fact that he is *distinct* from the others, *by appropriation* has his own activity in the history of salvation, has a relationship with creation, and, above all, has a relationship with humanity.

The differences in the actions of the three persons might be described in this way: everything comes from the Father, everything is accomplished and actualized by the Son, everything reaches humanity and becomes present to and experienced by humanity through the Holy Spirit. On the other hand, the return to God follows a reverse process: in the Spirit and through the Son we reach the Father. This is the basis of the liturgical prayer: "ad Patrem, per Filium, in Spiritu Sancto" ("to the Father through the Son in the Holy Spirit"). In this sense, it is always the Father who has the initiative in the history of salvation: everything proceeds from the person who *wants* to communicate to humanity his triune life. The Son acquiesces, that is, he *wants, along with the Father,* to be the one "in whom" and "through whom" the *project* or *plan* of the Father, that is, that union of God with humanity (and all creation) is accomplished. The Spirit, for his part, is the one who frees creation from its limits and renders it "capax Dei" ("capable of receiving God"; see St. Augustine, *On the Trinity,* 14, 8, 11). More simply, we can affirm that the Holy Spirit is the one who renders effective and accomplishes the actions of the Father and the Son through the history of salvation. This is all expressed by the Fathers with the classic formula: "all goodness descends from the Father, through the Son, [and it reaches us] in the Holy Spirit" (St. Athanasius, *Letter to Serapion,* I, 24). While the movement of God toward humanity is descending because it passes through Christ and reaches its objective in the Holy Spirit, the movement of humanity moves by an inverse dynamic and ascends: living in the Holy Spirit it rises, moves close to God, and through the Son has access to the Father.

In the same vein, St. Irenaeus (d. ca. 200) gives witness to the ancient tradition of the Church: "The priests and disciples of the apostles say that this is the order and rhythm of those who save us. Progress is by these steps: through the Holy Spirit people reach the Son and through the Son, the Father" (*Against Heresies,* V, 36, 2). And St. Basil the Great (d. 379) summarized the double trinitarian movement from the Father to us and from us to the Father: "The path to knowing God leads from the only Spirit through the only Son to the only Father. And, on the other hand, natural goodness and holiness according to nature and royal dignity flow from the Father through the Son to the Spirit" (*On the Holy Spirit,* XVIII, 47).

The divine economy is the common task of the three divine persons, committed to the same mission: to accompany humanity in the discovery of love, and to the understanding of who God is — God the basis of reality and the truth of being. "Being a work at once common and personal, the whole divine economy makes known both what is proper to the divine persons and their one divine nature. Hence the whole Christian life is a communion with each of the divine persons, without in any way separating them. Everyone who glorifies the Father does so through the Son in the Holy Spirit; everyone who follows Christ does so because the Father draws him and the Spirit moves him" (CCC, 259).

"In the Holy Spirit"

Before dealing with the various themes regarding the specific role of the Holy Spirit, let us pause over the significance of the expression "in the Spirit" because it will occur often in these pages. In summary, this expression means that the ineffable mystery of God becomes an experience for the believer only by the power of his Spirit. Through the Spirit, the invisible, ineffable and incommunicable God in his immense mercy draws near to people and becomes God among us: "But, as it is written, 'What no eye has seen, nor ear heard, nor the human heart conceived, what God has prepared for those who love him' — these things God has revealed to us through the Spirit; for the Spirit searches everything, even the depths of God. For what human being knows what is truly more human except the human spirit that is within? So also no one comprehends what is truly God's except the Spirit of God" (1 Cor. 2:9–11).

How does the Holy Spirit reveal the "depths of God"?

God Becomes, He Makes Himself, a "Gift" in the Spirit

John Paul II affirms: "In his intimate life, God 'is love,' the essential love shared by three divine persons: personal love is the Holy Spirit as the Spirit of the Father and the Son. Therefore, he 'searches even the depths of God,' as uncreated love-gift. It can be said that in the Holy Spirit the intimate life of the triune God becomes totally gift, an exchange of mutual love between the divine persons, and that through the Holy Spirit God exists in the mode of gift. It is the Holy Spirit who is the personal expression of this self-giving, of this being-love. He is person-love. He is person-gift. Here we have an inexhaustible treasure of the reality and an inexpressible deepening of the concept of person in God, which only divine revelation makes known to us" (*DeV*, 10).

The expression "in the Spirit," therefore, means above all that God in his immensity accepts each person and gives his "gift" through grace, uniting himself with that person. God remains totally Other, ineffable and incommunicable. But because he is *love-communion,* he finds a way to accomplish the unaccomplishable: to give himself to his creatures and unite himself to them. This is possible "in the Spirit" because the Spirit represents the eternal mutual love between the Father and the Son and their *being-in-communion*. This is also the role of the Spirit in the economy of salvation: God places himself in communion with his creatures "in the Spirit," and this "in the Spirit" fills the infinite distance which separates the uncreated from the created, God from human beings, and becomes God-for-us, God-with-us, and God-among-us. In this regard, St. Cyril of Jerusalem (d. 387) preferred the expression "with the Spirit" instead of "in the Spirit," in that God is engaged with humanity and makes his gift *with the Spirit:* "The Father bestows every grace on us through the Son and with the Spirit" (*Catecheses*, XVI, 24).

Therefore, no communication of God exists in his creatures if not "in the Spirit." For the same reasons we can also say that no experience of God and the things of God exists if not in the very same Spirit.

God Becomes a Living Experience through His Word in the Spirit

There can be no experience of God in the Scriptures if it is not *inspired* by the Spirit. "Sacred Scripture is the speech of God as it is put down in writing under the breath of the Holy Spirit" (*DV,* 9). Sacred Scripture, in that it is the Word of God directed to human beings, offers the possibility of encountering God in a vital and open dialogue. It is impossible that God's self-revelation in his Word come without the Spirit who renders visible the invisible and palpable the impalpable. Present in the Spirit is the unique dynamism that reaches the Son from the Father and from the Son in the Spirit reaches every human being. This means that the experience of God through his Word is given by the action of the Holy Spirit, who orients human beings toward the search for truth.

This idea is underscored several times in the New Testament. St. Peter, in saying that no prophecy in the Scripture can be the object of private interpretation, also reveals how no understanding of God can be made without the action of the Holy Spirit (see 2 Pet. 1:20). In turn, St. Paul teaches that "all Scripture is inspired by God" (2 Tim. 3:16) — using the technical term *theopneustos* (inspired by God) to indicate the special act by which God inspired the Scriptures — "useful for teaching, for reproof, for correction, and for training in righteousness, so that everyone who belongs to God may be proficient, equipped for every good work." Now these very functions of the Scripture seem to recall the action of the Spirit as the "mouth of God" as expressed by Simeon the New Theologian (d. 1022): "The mouth of God is the Holy Spirit and God's Word is his Son, also God. Why is the Spirit called the mouth of God and the Son, the Word? In the same way in which our interior speech goes out through our

mouth and is revealed to others — without a mouth there is
no other way in which we could articulate or manifest this
speech — the very Son and Word of God needs to be expressed or revealed by the Holy Spirit, as if by a mouth, or
he cannot be known or understood" (*Book of Ethics,* III).

In the Spirit the Word of God Becomes "Alive"

Furthermore, the inspiration which the Spirit exercises is not
limited to the moment of the Bible's birth, but also includes
assistance in *the very reading of the Bible.* The "coming to
life" of the Word of God is the work of the Holy Spirit:
the Bible would remain a dead letter if it were not currently
made forceful by the Holy Spirit. The Word is living through
the Spirit, who dwells in it in the same way as he rested over
the Son at the moment of the Son's baptism: "All the words
of God contained in Scripture... are full of the Holy Spirit,"
affirms St. Hilary of Poitiers (d. ca. 367, *Commentary on the
Psalms,* 118). These become a live and salvific reality thanks
to the action of the Spirit who is quietly received and welcomed because it is not possible "to understand without the
aid of the Holy Spirit" (St. Jerome, *Letters,* 120). According to William of Saint-Thierry (d. 1148): "The Scriptures
wish to be read through the very Spirit with which they were
written; and they must be understood through this method"
(*Golden Epistle,* 121).

Interpreting Scripture in the Spirit means interpreting it in
the light of faith, searching for its ultimate meaning. This
is possible only by never forgetting that Jesus Christ is the
unifying principle of all Scripture. Starting with Christ the
interpretation in the Spirit is inserted into the movement of
revelation and into the analogy of faith, which enhances the
coherence of revealed truth (see *CCC,* 114). In this way the
Holy Spirit acts so that the Word of God currently becomes
"Spirit and Life" and has the force to challenge and to cre-

ate communion among people. The Gospel of John (6:63) underscores how the action of the Word and that of the Spirit penetrate each other in turn. The Word *becomes flesh* (see John 1:14) while the function of the Spirit is *to make flesh.* The Spirit is the power of incarnation, of presence, of truth, and of acceptance: without him the Word remains ineffective, inoperative, exteriorized, and inconsistent.

At the same time, the Spirit prepares the human heart for listening, makes the heart capable and desirous of welcoming the Word. In this, the act of faith is a gift of the Spirit. People can believe by going out of themselves to entrust themselves to God, precisely because the Holy Spirit is the one who illuminates the revelation of God executed by Jesus. Belief is not a vague sentiment nor a pious desire. It is allowing God to accomplish, along with humanity, the history of salvation. For this reason, belief is a rational choice without which reality might remain confined to the absurd and each person incapable of understanding "his most high calling" (*GS, 22*).

The Word Speaks to Us Today in the Spirit

"We have become aware that the Spirit accompanies the Word," St. John Damascene (d. ca. 750) affirms (*On the Orthodox Faith,* 1, 7). For the Fathers of the Church it is necessary to live in receptiveness to the Spirit. This is necessary for belief in the inspiration of the Spirit and for succeeding in going beyond the sum of the facts of human history to achieve an understanding of the providential plan that sustains and guides history. The Fathers of Alexandria speak of a "spiritual" interpretation, which means, above all, interpretation "in the Spirit." For Origen (d. ca. 254), the true interpretation of the Scriptures is spiritual, that which "the Spirit gives to the Church" (*Homily on Leviticus,* V, 5), because "the entire law is spiritual. What the law wants to express spiritually is not known to all but only to those who have been given the grace of the Holy Spirit in their words of wisdom and knowledge" (*On First Principles,* preface, 8).

The Fathers insist on the need to read the Bible in Christ and from within his body, which is the Church. Only in this way can the divine Word echo with resonance today, similarly to the way it happened with the apostles, thanks to the Spirit of Truth which teaches everything (see John 14:26). "Let anyone who has an ear listen to what the Spirit is saying to the churches" (Rev. 3:6). The task of the Holy Spirit is to reveal Christ, to make him present.

God Addresses Us through His Church "in the Spirit"

The experience of God comes not only from the Word, but also from the tradition of the Church through its teaching, dogma, and religious instruction. Every understanding of God is a gift of the Spirit and comes true in the Spirit. According to John's Gospel, the function of the Spirit will be to introduce to believers the fullness of this truth and make it a vital part of their souls (John 16:13). Because of this, the Spirit is called "the Spirit *of truth*" (John 14:17; 15:26), as his action is ordered toward the truth which is Christ. "The Holy Spirit continually instructs the faithful to the degree in which each one is able to understand spiritual things. It also ignites an increasingly more vital desire in their hearts, which progresses in keeping with their charity, enabling them to love the things they already know and wish to know what they do not know" (St. Augustine, *Commentary on the Gospel of John,* 97, 1).

God Is "Known" Only If We Communicate with Him in the Spirit

"To know" God means to communicate with him through Jesus by means of the power operating in the Spirit: people truly "know" God in the measure to which they communicate with God. The biblical meaning of knowledge of God, in fact, regards the close personal contact between God and human beings, initiated at creation, renewed with the vocation of Israel, and completed in Christ. This is not an awareness understood solely as accepting news about God or participating in his knowledge. It is, rather, a relationship with God that the Spirit makes happen in the life of the believer. This is why people cannot know God without loving him, just as people cannot love him without knowing him. To think of God and love him is the same act of union. St. Gregory of Nazianzus is right in affirming: "There is no other way of knowing God for you except to live in him" (*Orations*, XXXII, 12).

In summary, *the supreme principle* and fundamental reference of all knowledge of God is always found in the "theology of the Spirit": knowing God means knowing him "in the Spirit." Simeon the New Theologian writes: "What is, in fact, the key to knowledge if not the grace of the Holy Spirit given through faith, which truly illuminates knowledge and full understanding? If the Holy Spirit is called key it is because, through him and in him, first of all, we have our *spirit* enlightened, and once purified we are illuminated with the light of knowledge and baptized from on high, born again (see John 3:3–5), and made sons of God" (*Catecheses*, XXXIII).

The Spirit puts the believer into vital contact with the Father through the Word to unite them and, thus, "to know" divinity. Therefore, the Christian can contemplate "with the eyes of the Holy Spirit the divinity which remains hidden in its epiphany" (Maximus the Confessor, *Ambigua*).

Conclusion

John Paul II's apostolic letter *Tertio Millennio Adveniente*, in referring to preparations for the Great Jubilee, affirms: "Especially in this phase, the phase of celebration, the aim will be to give glory to the Trinity, from whom everything in the world and in history comes and to whom everything returns. His mystery is the focus of the three years of immediate preparation: from Christ and through Christ, in the Holy Spirit, to the Father. In this sense the Jubilee celebration makes present in an anticipatory way the goal and fulfillment of the life of each Christian and of the whole Church in the triune God" (*TMA, 55*).

Rediscovering the importance of the Holy Spirit means to accept the meaning of the salvation that the Father and the Son have offered to humanity. It is impossible to have any contact with God if not in the Spirit: to live in the Spirit simply means to be Christian, to believe and "to know" the God revealed by Jesus Christ. "To discover" the Spirit and make him known in this Jubilee simply means "to evangelize" people.

The Great Jubilee could constitute a privileged time to live "in the Spirit" and rediscover the Christian vocation. This implies letting ourselves be divinely transfigured, living in obedience to the will of God with the knowledge of his will and turning the law of love into a reality. Returning to the primacy of the Word for the life of the Church means understanding the unsurpassed truth of the redemption accomplished by Christ twenty centuries ago. It was freely offered even for the people of today, crushed by the weight of skepticism and weary of the quest. If the Spirit is the place for experiencing God-in-us and God-for-us, living within this memory for the Christian means to adopt the disturbing originality of the paschal mystery: a mystery of reconciliation, salvation, and freedom from sin. This is the experience "in the Spirit" to which every believer is called: be open to his action because in the witness of love-communion "those far away" come closer to the source of redemption and freedom and the marginalized live in the "house" of God, who is the Spirit of love and consolation.

Chapter 2

The Spirit and Creation

The often recalled principle that "everything proceeds from the Father through the Son and in the Spirit" takes this "everything" back to the *creation of the universe.* Creation is understood as the call on the part of God for new existence from non-being, that is, from nothing to being. This call marks the start of the history of salvation, in other words the start of God's self-communication with his creatures. It is routinely affirmed that "God" created all beings through a free and loving act of his will. But in saying that "God" created does not embrace all the salvific richness and significance of creation. It is necessary to be more precise: "The Father created everything that exists outside of the divinity through his Word in the power of the Spirit."

The faith of the Church in the "creator Spirit" is attested to in the *creeds* and in liturgical texts. The Creed professes: "We believe in the Holy Spirit, the Lord, the giver of life." The Third Eucharistic Prayer says: "Through Jesus Christ your Son, our Lord, in the power of the Holy Spirit bring to life and sanctify the universe." Another liturgical text says: "Come Holy Spirit, fill the hearts of your faithful and kindle in them the fire of your love. Send forth your Spirit and the face of the earth will be renewed." The most popular hymn to the Holy Spirit sings: "Veni, creator Spiritus" ("Come, creator Spirit"). The Byzantine liturgy often refers to the creative work of the Spirit: "It belongs to the Holy Spirit to rule, sanctify, and animate creation, for he is God consubstantial with the Father and the Son....Power over life pertains to the Spirit, for being God he preserves creation in the Father through the Son" (Sundays of the second mode, Troparion of Morning Prayer; in *CCC*, 703).

God the Father Creates through the Word in the Power of the Spirit

The Church believes that God creates everything, giving existence and life through Christ *in* the Spirit. And it is in the Holy Spirit that God the Father — in loving *ek-stasis* ("emerging from himself") — "transcends" his unearthly life and makes room for his creatures. The Holy Spirit is the divine person through which God the Father immediately animates life. He is the final "touch" through which God unites with his creatures, saves them from non-existence, sustains them, renews them, and directs them toward their fulfillment. Being in the Spirit equals being in "life."

On the basis of these indications, we understand why the Hebrew term for spirit, *ruach*, lets us foresee in the experience of the people of Israel and in the "Christian" rereading of the text, a fundamental connection between Spirit and life. The term "Spirit" means more than its immediate etymological meanings (breath, blowing, wind). It indicates a life-giving force, the energy at work in these actions. Let us underscore that the *ruach* acts at a cosmic and historical level, showing the originality of Old Testament revelation. It is the "breath" of God that allows the realization of salvation history from the beginning of creation.

In the Old Testament, God creates through his *word* and *action* (see Gen. 1:7–16; 25–26). But his *breath*, his *ruach*, will be the protagonist of creation: "When you hide your face, they are dismayed; when you take away their breath, they die and return to their dust. When you send forth your spirit, they are created; and you renew the face of the ground" (Ps. 104:29–30). In Psalm 33:6 there is a clear parallelism between the *word* and the *breath* (*ruach*) of God the creator: "By the word of the Lord the heavens were made, and all their host by the breath of his mouth." This is the context used by biblical scholars to interpret the expression in Genesis 1:1–2: "In the beginning when God created the heavens and the earth, the earth was a formless void and darkness covered the face of the deep, while a wind from God [*ruach Elohim*] swept over the face of the waters." It is also the context for understanding the pleasure expressed by God in Genesis (1:4) regarding creation. In this way, the Holy Spirit not only sustains the cosmos in freedom and love against all destructive and chaotic powers but also constitutes the very power of the new creation, which is awaited in messianic hope by a people with a new heart (see Ezek. 37:1–14; Joel 3:1ff.).

The New Testament announces the definitive fulfillment of the creative power with which God works in the world and in history. The historical event of Jesus Christ marks the beginning of freedom; in his Spirit the reality of the new creation is present. This Spirit is the giver of life (see John 6:63; 1 Cor. 15:45).

The Christians of the first centuries were especially sensitive to this truth. The example referred to frequently by St. Irenaeus in his work *Against Heresies*, written between 180 and 185, has remained famous: "God has created the world with his two hands, the Son and the Spirit" (*Against Heresies*, 4, 4, 4; 4, 7, 4; 5, 1, 3; 5, 5, 1). St. Basil underscored that the specific work of the Spirit in creation is that of *perfecting* it and *confirming* it: "You could have learned of the communion of the Spirit with the Father and with the Son from the initial act of creation.... The Father, since he creates by his very will, would not have needed the Son; but he wants to create through the Son. The Son would not even have needed cooperation, since he acts in the same way as the Father, but even the Son wanted to perfect the work through the Spirit.... You understand, therefore, that there are three: the Lord who orders, the Word who creates, the Breath who confirms. Who else could have been the confirmation if not the one who perfects?" (*On the Holy Spirit,* XVI, 38). Western tradition, too, has a strong awareness of the creating role of the Spirit. St. Ambrose (d. 397) affirms that the Scriptures "have not only taught that without the Spirit no creature could endure, but even that the Spirit is the creator of every creature. Who could deny that the creation of the earth was the work of the Holy Spirit? Who could deny that, if the creation of the earth was the work of the Holy Spirit, then its renewal is also the work of the Spirit?...Do we believe that without the work of the Holy Spirit the substance of the earth would exist when without his action not even the vaults of heaven exist?" (*On the Holy Spirit,* II, 34–35).

The *Catechism of the Catholic Church* summarizes this teaching: "The Word of God and his Breath are at the origin of the being and life of every creature" (CCC, 703). It is the oft-repeated principle of the divine economy. "The Father creates and renews everything through the Word in the Spirit' (St. Athanasius, *Letter to Serapion,* I, 24). As St. Athanasius further said: "All creation participates in the Word in the Spirit" (ibid).

The Salvific Meaning of Creation in the Spirit

The theological affirmation of creation in the Spirit means that creation is marked by divine goodness. In the intratrinitarian life, the Spirit is the eternal link between Father and Son. Analogously, with regard to creation the Holy Spirit acts so that every creature can experience the essential mystery of life: the communion of human beings with God, with others, and with all of reality. This is what motivates the salvific meaning of creation: God creates starting from a plan of salvation into which human beings are introduced in order to contemplate the very life of the Trinity.

In this sense, the salvific value of creation is twofold. First of all at an anthropological level: if the self-communication of God is the motive for creation, it is because "glorification" constitutes the ultimate good for human beings, who are called to seek their proper identity. The Holy Spirit accompanies people in this fundamental choice for their happiness. Free to accept that identity or reject it, they know that "without a creator there can be no creature" (*GS*, 36). It is the great mystery of creation: "We believe that God created the world according to his wisdom. It is not the product of any necessity whatever, nor of blind fate or chance. We believe that it proceeds from God's free will; he wanted to make his creatures share in his being, wisdom, and goodness" (*CCC*, 295).

Second of all at a cosmological level: the world participates in the goodness of God and exists in God. Outside of him nothing has a reason for being. The cosmos is more than the scenery for the revelation of the God-Man. It is also the *meaningful word* in that its existence reveals God's will to communicate with creatures. The task of the Spirit in this act of creation continues and is twofold: on the one hand, he currently constitutes the ultimate foundation for the existence of the universe because without him that which has been created returns to non-being; on the other hand, he assigns to creation its significance of being the *glory* of God, that is, the revelation of the omnipotent love of God, rendering it a meaningful "word" and an act in a relationship.

John Paul II summarizes this vision of the tradition of the Church in his apostolic letter *Dominum et Vivificantem:*

" 'The *Spirit of God,*' who according to the biblical description of creation 'was moving over the face of the water,' signifies the same 'Spirit who searches the depth of God': searches the depths of the Father and of the Word-Son in the mystery of creation. Not only is he the direct witness of their mutual love from which creation derives, but he himself is this love. He himself, as love, is the eternal uncreated gift. In him is the source and the beginning of every giving of gifts to creatures. The witness concerning the beginning, which we find in the whole of revelation, beginning with the Book of Genesis, is unanimous on this point. To create means to call into existence from nothing: therefore, to create means to give existence" (*DeV,* 34).

Creation Is "Good," Existing in the Spirit and for the Spirit

If creation, as the Fathers say, is the word of God made into reality, we can understand how it owes its existence to the contemporary action of the Holy Spirit. This means that the world exists in virtue of the creator Spirit. Creation, in its birth and in its continuance, is profoundly "spiritual." This explains the saying that "it is good" (Gen. 1:10), an expression which simultaneously means good and beautiful. Creation in the Spirit, in this way, becomes a manifestation of the "Word" through which and for which the Father created the universe: "All things came into being through him," that is, through the Word, as John affirms in the Prologue of his Gospel (1:3).

The decisive aspect of the Christian concept of creation is found here: the fullness of revelation in Jesus Christ opens a more profound understanding of what was in the Old Testament "in principle." The unconditional love and benevolence of the original plan, in which the first creation forms the

stage for the "new creation" accomplished by Christ at his
second coming (*parousia*), find their ultimate meaning starting with Jesus, the "first" in the design of the Father. All
God's creating acts are to be read in the light of the creation in the Son, in which every person is called to a new
and eternal covenant. It is in Christ that we have been chosen and saved from the beginning, and it is the same Christ
who frees us from sin in the paschal mystery, the new and
true creation. The New Testament, in fact, underscores that
Jesus is the mediator and finality of all creation. Even more,
it gives evidence that creation and salvation gain in Christ a
profound unity, in the very mystery of the resurrection: with
this all of history is open to the future of God, whose meaning is the offering of salvation to all people. "The Word of
God, through whom all things were made, was made flesh,
so that as a perfect man he could save all of human history,
the focal point of the desires of history and civilization, the
center of mankind, the joy of all hearts, and the fulfillment
of all aspirations. It is he whom the Father raised from the
dead, exalted, and placed at his right hand, constituting him
judge of the living and the dead. Animated and drawn together in his Spirit we press onwards on our journey towards
the consummation of history which fully corresponds to the
plan of love: 'to gather up all things in him, things in heaven
and things on earth' (Eph. 1:10)" (*GS*, 45).

From this viewpoint, we can understand why the Fathers
of the Church cite Genesis 1:10 and John 1:3 to affirm the
goodness and beauty of the universe (see St. Basil, *Homilies
on the Hexaemeron*, III, 10), which derive from the wisdom
of God, creator of the world. This beauty is spread in the
world by the Spirit. St. Ambrose engaged in polemics against
those who denied the divinity of the Spirit and affirmed that
the Spirit not only cooperates with the Father and the Son in
creating the world, but is the one who, as the divine artist,

puts "order" in the world and renders it "beautiful": "Can we doubt that the Holy Spirit vitalizes every thing, from the moment when he, along with the Father and the Son, is creator of all things and that we must think that the omnipotent God the Father performed everything with the Holy Spirit, because even at the beginning of creation *the Spirit swept over the face of the water?* (Gen. 1:2). So, at the time the Spirit was about to move, creation had no beauty. Instead, the creation of this world, receiving the Spirit's work, merited all this attractive beauty of a resplendent world" (*On the Holy Spirit*, II, 32).

The Fathers, therefore, tended to see the world as a "theophany," a sign of God's presence and beauty. This involves a true and proper "sacramental cosmology" in which the world is considered "sacred." This signifies for the ancient tradition of the Church that the world is a "mystery," that is, a sacrament, a signifying reality which refers back to him whom it signifies. But it is necessary to see the sense of this mystery because, as an ancient Church writer says: "We note that everything is full of mystery" (Origen, *Homily on Leviticus*, III, 8). As is the case with reading the Bible, the intervention of the Spirit is necessary to "decode" the world and see with the "spiritual senses" the mystery hidden in the Word. The action of the Spirit is necessary because only through his grace is this possible. As Maximus the Confessor would say: "The prodigious and ineffable fire hidden in the essence of things as in the burning bush is the fire of divine love and the flashing splendor of his [God's] beauty within all things" (*Ambigua*).

Contemplating nature constitutes a great help in nourishing in us the "remembrance of God." This is an expression which for the ancient authors meant having that sweet and subtle perception of the surrounding and involving presence of God in life and history, perceived also through the signs of his work of creation. St. Basil said: "I want to awake in you a deep admiration for creation, until you in every place, contemplating plants and flowers, are overcome by a living remembrance of the Creator" (*Homilies on the Hexaemeron*, VI, 1).

In Church tradition the world represents a theophany and is "contemplated" to discover God. This involves a religious contemplation of creation practiced by the "spiritual senses," those new senses given to Christians by the Spirit to understand the divine traces hidden in every being, that is, the wisdom and goodness of God the creator who forged everything through his Word. Only in this case can we overcome the exteriority of things and "feel" their true language. It constitutes the true "knowledge" of things through which Christians, purified and with their "pure hearts" regained, can catch sight of the "divine plan" and discover the divine providence made of love and Wisdom. Then does nature truly become an "open book" capable of making known God and his design of love.

Conclusion

The world, sign of God's benevolence and the progressive manifestation of the Word through the action of the Spirit, is also the expression of a declining, devastated, and oppressed creation waiting for that final liberation that only the *new creation* in Christ can accomplish. Human beings, in fact, "turned in upon themselves," are continually tempted to become closed to the action of the Spirit, constantly put creation in danger, and tend to hide the "goodness" of the world which resides in its existence "in the Spirit." On the contrary, creation is a reality open to the salvific plan of God to which every person is called to cooperation in transforming the world into a hospitable and communal place. The action of the Holy Spirit is necessary to sustain the world's goodness and favor its development. Coming to help us in "our weakness" (Rom. 8:26) is the Spirit, who prevents us from snuffing out his creative action and who, inspiring hope in a new creation, aids in the work of preserving creation.

Given all this, the Great Jubilee could represent an occasion for discovering that the world is involved in Christ's redemption. Given the violent ideology of the myth of progress, people's desire for power makes them think they can reduce the world to exploitable energy deposits without any respect for the rhythms and balance of nature. This is not the case in the Christian vision of the world. The meaning of the creation story (see Gen. 2:15) is in humanity's safeguarding and taking care of that which has been created. This responsibility plunges people's roots into the salvific dimension of creation itself. The aim of creation is to make possible the history of the covenant between God and humanity, which reaches its culmination at Easter: the world finds its consistency in God. If the world is "hidden with Christ in God" (Col. 3:3), then all of reality is not the exclusive domain of humanity, but a network of relationships in which every creature is sustained and nourished by triune love. Because of this, the responsibility of humanity for the world is an ethical choice in which all are is committed to give an accounting to the Creator for their own relationship with nature. The Spirit is in action to redeem creation even if, for the moment, it "groans and suffers the labor pains of birth" along with humanity, awaiting the complete and definitive redemption (see Rom. 8:22). The love for creation (ecology) does not stem from a simple aesthetic admiration or from the usefulness that can be derived from it or from the necessity to save the "ecosystem." It is found in concern for the extinction of the very existence of humanity.

Creatures are no less than the fruit of God's call to existence in order to realize the goal of full communion with all things, including their Creator. The fact that the world has a purpose presupposes that among created beings there exist those with their own conscience and freedom. Among all the creatures, only human beings are free and therefore only they can become, in Christ, through the power of the Spirit, the *mediator* in achieving the destiny of the world. Human beings are the priests of the cosmos because only they are able to return to God as created beings for a personal encounter with him as a conscious response to him who, with his Word and Spirit, sustains humanity. All creatures, through human beings, thus achieve the destiny of their existence. Because of this, human beings are in a mysterious communion with God, not only because they are the free and loving fruit of his goodness but also because they have the vocation to respond freely with love to the creative word of God given to all creatures. They, "made the voice of every creature," become the cosmic priests who praise the Lord "for all his creatures."

With Alyosha Karamazov we might say: "My brothers, love creation in its entirety and in its elements: every leaf, every sunbeam, the animals, the plants. And loving everything you shall understand the divine mystery of things. Once understood, you will comprehend it better every day. And you will end by loving the whole world in a universal love" (Fyodor Dostoyevsky, *The Brothers Karamazov*). St. Francis of Assisi (d. 1226) prayed: "Be thou praised, my Lord, with all thy creatures, above all Brother Sun, who gives the day and lightens us therewith. And he is beautiful, and radiant with great splendor; of thee, most high, he bears similitude" (*Canticle of the Sun*).

Chapter 3

The Spirit
and Humanity

The Spirit, along with the Father and the Son, is the origin and support of all creation, so it can be affirmed that each human being is a true and proper *locus theologicus*. Through the omnipotent Word of the Father, each human becomes a being from non-being and is blessed with intelligence and the ability to love, notwithstanding human instability because of sin. The Spirit breathed by God into human nostrils instills life. After sin, it is the Spirit who transmits the new life ransomed by Christ. The Spirit always incarnates and stamps in human beings the image of God. In this regenerative work, each human becomes a "child in the Son."

The doctrine on the Spirit "is true first of all concerning man, who has been created in the image and likeness of God: 'Let us make him in our image, after our likeness.' 'Let us make': Can one hold that the plural which the creator uses here in speaking of himself already in some way suggests the Trinitarian mystery, the presence of the Trinity in the work of the creation of man? The Christian reader, who already knows the revelation of this mystery, can discern a reflection of it also in these words. At any rate, the context of the Book of Genesis enables us to see in the creation of man the first beginning of God's salvific self-giving commensurate with the 'image and likeness' of himself which he has granted to man" (*DeV*, 12).

Humanity Is "Spiritual" by the Work of the Spirit and in the Spirit

"Moses," writes Cyril of Alexandria (d. 444) "recounts that God, during creation, breathed the breath of life unto the face of man. Man is recreated today similarly to the way in which he was created in the beginning. Now, as then, he is remade to the likeness of his Creator by the Holy Spirit" (*Commentary on Exodus*, II).

Scripture and Church tradition teach that each human is alive due to the current action of the Spirit. This is why each human is "spiritual" only in the Spirit of God, who represents for humans the principle of life. In Christian terminology, speaking of the "spiritual life" of humanity does not refer simply to a superior life in opposition to the corporal and biological one, but precisely to "life in the Spirit." Each person is "spiritual" and lives in the Spirit and for the Spirit of God, who is our final destination and fullness. "The Union of body and soul, receiving the Spirit of God, constitutes the spiritual man," affirms St. Irenaeus (*Against Heresies*, V, 8, 2). The concept is explained more clearly in the same work: "These are the men the Apostle calls spiritual (1 Cor. 2:15; 3:1). They are spiritual, thanks to their participation in the Spirit and not because of any privation or erasing of the flesh" (*Against Heresies*, V, 6, 1).

By grace, the Holy Spirit belongs to the "spiritual" structure of each person. This outlook explains why the Church mystics affirm that the Holy Spirit is "the soul of the human soul." This, however, must not lead to the belief that the soul and the Holy Spirit are identical. The Holy Spirit is always a gift, a grace given to humanity by God the Father. He constitutes the way in which humanity participates in the nature of God through creation and transmits the re-creation brought about by Christ. How is the gift of the Holy Spirit expressed? It is expressed in rendering each creature "capax Dei," constantly willing to see God. "Man was made to see God: to this end God made his creature rational, so that he could participate in his likeness, which consists in the vision of God" (Thomas Aquinas, *On Truth*, q. 18 a. 1,5). Humanity, at its roots, is characterized by this desire and is rendered capable of turning toward the communion-vision with God, but is always free to refuse. This desire to see God is inscribed in humanity, but let us not forget that the possibility to respond to this unique invitation of God is not founded on the exigency of humanity, but in the encounter between the free gift of the Trinity and the constitutive expectation of humanity. Because of this, the Holy Spirit acts to allow humanity to freely respond to the free gift of God. Hans Urs von Balthasar, a great Catholic theologian, gave a contemporary explanation of this intimate penetration of the entire person by the Spirit. "Our most intimate acts of faith, love, and hope, the dispositions of our spirit and feelings, our most personal and free resolutions: all these unmistakable realities which form us are interlaced in such a way by his breath, that the final subject — at the heart of our subjectivity — is him [the Spirit]" (from the essay "The Unknown beyond the Word," in *Spiritus Creator*).

The Fathers always sought to explain why it could be possible that God and the human being form a whole in the Spirit. St. Basil maintains that the Holy Spirit is the form or potency which worked in believers, directing them to the fullness of human and Christian maturity in their relationship with God. "He who no longer lives according to the flesh but is led by the Spirit of God and is called son of God, made in the image of the Son of God, is called spiritual. As the capacity to see resides in a healthy eye, so does the operating force of the Spirit exist in a purified soul" (*On the Holy Spirit*, XXVI, 61).

The Spirit Imprints the Image of God in Humanity

To answer the question "what is man?" the Fathers of the Church turned to the biblical expression "man is made in the image and likeness of God" (see Gen. 1:26; 2:7). This "made in the image of God" includes man and woman and is part of their structure. (The divine image is not something added to humanity, but *is* humanity itself.) God did not first make humanity and then add his image: each person is the image of God. But the true image of God is Christ (Col. 1:15–18). Humanity is the "icon of icons" and thus the image of Christ, who, in turn, is the incarnate image of the Father. The *Catechism of the Catholic Church* says: "It is in Christ, 'the image of the invisible God,' that man has been created 'in the image and likeness' of the creator. It is in Christ, Redeemer and Savior, that the divine image, disfigured in man by the first sin, has been restored to its original beauty and ennobled by the grace of God" (CCC, 1701).

What does it mean to be created in Christ, "in the image of the invisible God"? Revelation shows that God awakened a special self-awareness in humanity: in knowing our limits and desires, we simultaneously notice that that which we might be and wish to be is beyond our capabilities and that it is almost impossible to walk the true path of freedom. The incarnation takes place in Jesus Christ allowing God to radically approach humanity and himself become a man, allowing humanity to achieve self-realization in a communion-belonging with God. This logic provides the newness of Christian anthropology. "Christ's life gives us a new understanding of God and of man. As 'the God of Christians' is new and specific, so 'the man of the Christians' is new and original regarding other concepts of man" (International Theological Commission, "Questioni di cristologia," *Enchiridion Vaticanum,* 7, 662).

Christological revelation opens new paths in the understanding of humanity. On one hand, the Christ event shows how the truth about humanity — despite its likeness to God — is in its being different from God. The human being is not an absolute. Furthermore, when people try to organize their existence on the false image of their unconditional autonomy, they think of themselves as gods unto themselves and think of God as a projection of themselves. On the other hand, Jesus reveals that only in the encounter with the Other, the triune God, can each human being achieve self-understanding as a person in the dimension of sonship, in which the secret of reciprocity and of grace is found. "Being in the image of God the human individual possesses the dignity of a person, who is not just something, but someone. He is capable of self-knowledge, of self-possession, and of freely giving himself and entering into communion with other persons. And he is called by grace to a covenant with his Creator, to offer him a response of faith and love that no other creature can give in his stead" (CCC, 357).

If the human individual is psychosomatically structured in this fashion, it is because Christ is like this. From both the religious and the natural points of view, everything that human beings are derives from their nature as images of God in Christ. The possibility of being a person and of loving, of being a conscious individual within time and space, of being a psychosomatic entity with an unimaginable depth of freedom, intelligence, and creativity depends on the primordial, ontological relationship of each person with the archetype, the Lord Christ.

The image of each person came out of God's hands pure, was disfigured by sin, but has been restored by Christ with his death and resurrection. Redemption, in fact, means restoration of the divine image of humanity. Christian reality, the Church, the sacraments, and disciplines aim to transform people more into the image of Christ, to transform them more into the "new creature" in Christ. He is the savior of humanity because he frees from sin and perfects each person's image as a symbol of God. This is the primary objective of the incarnation, the "deification" of humanity. When the Fathers want to define the nature of humanity, they do not use the Aristotelian definition: "Man is a rational animal." They use the theological one: "He is a living being capable of becoming divine" (Gregory of Nazianzus, *Orations,* XLV, 7).

The Eastern and Western traditions of the Church are unanimous in affirming that the Holy Spirit stamps the image of God in each individual. He is considered the "iconographer" (the one who paints the sacred icon) of the image of God in each human because, with Christ as a model, he paints the living image of the Redeemer in each person and in this manner increasingly Christifies the faithful (see Pseudo-Macarius, *Homilies,* XXX, 4). The principle is always the same: God becomes present in each individual through Jesus Christ in the Holy Spirit; each human is the image of God because each is called to communion with God, and the Spirit is the one who causes the communion. This tie is not an external or psychological event, but transforms the very being of the person. Humanity since creation is called to this communion, which means "to be called to the image of God" through Jesus Christ in the Holy Spirit. St. Ambrose, revisiting 1 Cor. 15:49 affirms: "The Holy Spirit reproduces in us the outline of the heavenly image. Who dares to say that the Spirit is separated from God the Father and from Christ? Through him we merit being in the image and likeness of God, for it is through him that there takes place what the apostle Peter calls our participation in the divine nature (see 2 Pet. 1:4)" (*On the Holy Spirit,* I, 79–80).

Cyril of Alexandria, wanting to explain how humanity participates in the holiness of God, says: "We were created in the divine image. Sanctification produced this image in us, that is, our participation in Christ in the Spirit. This image was deformed when human nature fell into perversion. We return to our original state thanks to the Holy Spirit, who once again fuses us to the image of him who created us or, as might be better said, to the Son from whom everything comes to us through the Father" (*On the Trinity*, VI).

The action of the Spirit in forming the image of the Son in human beings is tied to the very creation of humanity and, after the fall, with the "re-creation" or "re-generation" which restores us to the original state. All this is truly done in a way that touches on our very nature.

Now we perceive the primary role the Holy Spirit plays in the formation of each human being: each person in the Holy Spirit becomes a living theology, a splendid manifestation of God because each human being "participates in the light and power of the divine Spirit" (CCC, 1704). Given these premises, the consequences for humanity are immense: "And if the visible world is created for man, therefore the world is given to man. And at the same time that same man in his own humanity receives as a gift a special 'image and likeness' to God. This means not only rationality and freedom as constitutive properties of human nature, but also, from the very beginning, the capacity to have a personal relationship with God as "I" and "you," and therefore the capacity to have a covenant, which will take place in God's salvific communication with man. Against the background of the 'image and likeness' of God, 'the gift of the Spirit' ultimately means a call to friendship in which the transcendent 'depths of God' become in some way opened to participation on the part of man" (*DeV*, 34).

Conclusion

Our starting point is one of the most beautiful pages of the encyclical *Dominum et Vivificantem*. The reflection it contains makes evident the intimate union of the Spirit with humanity and its role in revealing the mystery of God. "The Great Jubilee...ought to constitute a powerful call to all those who 'worship God in spirit and truth.' It should be for everyone a special occasion for meditating on the mystery of the triune God, who in himself is wholly transcendent with regard to the world, especially the visible world. For he is absolute Spirit, 'God is spirit,' and also, in such a marvelous way, he is not only close to this world but present in it and giving it life from within. This is especially true in relation to man" (*DeV*, 54).

This contains the profound truth about each person: to be made in the image of the Trinity, "able to receive God," open to relationships with oneself, others, and God. We all must search for this truth with the help of the Spirit and assimilate it as the fundamental choice of our existence. The life given by the Spirit is not a magical or mysterious process, but an event composed of acceptance and response. "Therefore, if you want to live in the Holy Spirit, preserve charity, love truth, wish for unity, and you will be united with eternity," said St. Augustine (*Sermons*, 267, 4, 4).

This means that each person is not free unless living in communion with God. Who can doubt, as the Church believes and professes, that in this divine encounter human existence experiences envelopment in an unconditional love. The Holy Spirit is the resting place of human freedom, the interpreter of this hope inscribed in the depths of the heart, which invites us not to contradict humanity's openness to the absolute and transcendent mystery of God. "The Spirit, therefore, is at the very source of man's existential and religious questioning, which is occasioned not only by contingent situations, but by the very structure of his being" (*RM*, 28). In this mystery, humanity discovers that being called to freedom is the great gift of the Father, the Son, and the Spirit — accomplished in the exercise of charity, that is, in the building of a civilization of love, respect, and solidarity in which an outgoing charity becomes the center of Christian life in the commitment to God and neighbor. Given this outlook, one of the main goals of the Great Jubilee is to make each person discover that authentic human dignity is not a contractual object but a free choice between the truth of God and the false affirmations of history. To think of finding happiness and the meaning of life without God means to be deluded into thinking you are freer and lighter, even though the marks of presumed human autonomy are the marks of violence, death, and suffering. However, if human beings live a "spiritual" life, that is, in God and according to God, they will realize who they really are and expand their being beyond themselves into the unfathomable depths of God, who already is leading people to "eternal life." "The dignity of this life is linked not only to its beginning, to the fact that it comes from God, but also to its final end, to its destiny of fellowship with God in knowledge and love of him. In the light of this truth St. Irenaeus qualifies and completes his praise of man: 'The glory of God,' is indeed, 'man, living man,' but 'the life of man consists in the vision of God' (*Against Heresies*, IV, 20, 7)" (*EV*, 38). Theophilus of Antioch (second century), asked by his Greek friend Autolycus to "show me your god!" answered: "Show me your man and I will show you my God!" (*To Autolycus*, I, 2). He meant: become a true man and see how you will find the true God.

Consequently, biological life is not enough for human beings. It cannot fulfill the search for love and freedom. The Gospel message, instead, underscores that "to live in the

Chapter 4

The Holy Spirit and Christ

The Great Jubilee has more than a christological profile. It is has a pneumatological one (see *DeV*, 50). The Spirit is precisely the personal place where humanity finds possible its encounter with Christ. The unique mediation of Christ, by which every human being can be introduced to the inaccessible intimacy of the Father, takes place through the experience of the Holy Spirit. From this follows the impossibility of distinguishing the task of the Son from the mission of the Spirit: as the Son makes evident the role of the Spirit in the self-communication of God and in the response of faith, so does the Spirit become the protagonist of the preparation and coming of the Word in history. Put in another way, the Spirit reveals nothing of himself in an independent way but only in relationship with the Word of life. This is his action which "has been exercised in every place and at every time, indeed, in every individual, according to the eternal plan of salvation whereby this action was to be closely linked with the mystery of the incarnation and redemption" (*DeV*, 53).

Knowing Christ, therefore, within the horizon of the Spirit means basing the wisdom of the faith on the experience, in the Spirit, of the mystery of the Word made flesh: "No one can say, 'Jesus is Lord' except by the Holy Spirit" (1 Cor. 12:3).

Jesus Possesses the Spirit

The original and unique relationship between Christ and the Spirit is the new element which characterizes the New Testament's outlook. The Spirit is the Spirit of Christ, and is the premise and the means for understanding the triune God. The Spirit has been entrusted with the mission of updating throughout time the loving design of God. God, starting with the creation of the universe, especially by creating human beings in the "image and likeness of God," and "speaking through the prophets," progressively makes known the Logos of God in history. Yet, it is the Spirit who brings about the culmination of God's self-communication, with the humanizing of the Son of God in the womb of the Virgin Mary (see Luke 1:35). The biological beginning of Christ is due to the Spirit. This is why we confess in the Creed that Christ was born "by the power of the Holy Spirit." The design of God, that of uniting himself with humanity and making it divine, is fully realized in Jesus. Because of this, we can affirm that Jesus, in the power of the Spirit, is the perfect union between God and humankind: "In the mystery of the incarnation the work of the Spirit 'who gives life' reaches its highest point. It is not possible to give life, which in its fullest form is in God, except by making it the life of man, as Christ is in his humanity endowed with personhood by the Word in the hypostatic union. And at the same time, with the mystery of the incarnation there opens in a new way the source of this divine life in the history of mankind: the Holy Spirit. The word, 'the firstborn of all creation,' becomes 'the firstborn of many brethren.' And thus he also becomes the head of the body which is the Church, which will be born on the cross and revealed on the day of Pentecost — and in the Church, he becomes the head of humanity: of the people of every nation, every race, every country and culture, every language and continent, all called to salvation. 'The Word became flesh, [that Word in whom] was life and the life was the light of men. . . . To all who received him he gave the power to become the children of God.' But all this was accomplished and is unceasingly accomplished 'by the power of the Holy Spirit'" (*DeV*, 52).

The New Testament points out two fundamental stages in the relationship between the Spirit and Christ: before Easter the Spirit is given to Christ; after his death and resurrection Jesus gives the gift of the Spirit, inaugurating the eschatological era of the Church's pilgrimage in history. Based on this, we can say that Jesus Christ, the Word of God incarnate, concretely exists in history by work of the Spirit. From conception Christ is anointed by the Spirit. But it is in his baptism that this anointing is shown in its truest reality: Christ is constituted as Son of God for us and for our salvation. He is the messiah. This investiture and consecration of Jesus by the Spirit is clearly expressed by St. Peter in his speech to Cornelius: "That message spread throughout Judea, beginning in Galilee after the baptism that John announced: how God anointed Jesus of Nazareth with the Holy Spirit and with power; how he went about doing good and healing all who were oppressed by the devil, for God was with him" (Acts 10:37–38).

From now on, every action of Jesus will only be an "actualization," for the power of the Spirit will lead the Savior, almost by the hand, toward his work of salvation. Thus, the first act of the Spirit after the baptism will be to "lead" Jesus into the desert to combat and overcome the devil (see Matt. 4:1–11 and parallel accounts). The Holy Spirit will be seen in the public life of Jesus as the power of freedom from the force of evil, as in the miracles. The Spirit announces and gives witness to the finality and uniqueness of revelation in Jesus (see Luke 4:18–21; John 3:34). The evangelist Luke, in particular, will express this relationship between the Spirit and Jesus in his prayer to the Father. The Hymn of Jubilee, as this prayer has come to be called, is introduced by the evangelist with the words: "At that same hour Jesus rejoiced in the Holy Spirit" (Luke 10:21), thereby testifying that, in his relationship with the Father, the Spirit is always present.

The Holy Spirit is present above all at the moment of Christ's death. According to the letter to the Hebrews (9:14–15), the Holy Spirit brought forth the sacrificial offering of Christ in his redeeming death, in which the motivating force of the true sacrifice consists in the offering Christ makes of himself. Christ "offers himself" to God through the generous compliance of his will (see Heb. 10:4–10), and this comes through the impulse and with the strength of the Holy Spirit who inspired and sustained the sacrifice of Christ because the Spirit is the origin of Christ's charity toward God and toward his brethren.

In the resurrection of Jesus as well the operating force of the Spirit is present and effective. True, it is the Father who raises Jesus (see Rom. 8:11; 1 Cor. 6:14), but this takes place through the Holy Spirit: "he was put to death in the flesh, but made alive in the Spirit" (1 Pet. 3:18). This takes place also for our resurrection, which is a direct consequence of Christ's resurrection (see Rom. 8:11). "The messianic 'raising up' of Christ in the Holy Spirit reaches its zenith in the resurrection, in which he reveals himself also as the Son of God, 'full of power' " (*DeV*, 24). The Spirit that gave birth to Christ is the same who raised him up from the dead and constitutes him as the "final Adam," the definitive human being, making him, in turn, "a life-giving spirit" (1 Cor. 15:45).

The Crucified-Resurrected One Bestows the Spirit

During his earthly life, at the festival of the tabernacles, Jesus promised to give the gift of the Spirit to believers after the resurrection: "Let anyone who is thirsty come to me, and let the one who believes in me drink. As the Scripture has said, 'Out of the believer's heart shall flow rivers of living water' "

(John 7:37–38). The Gospel writer comments: "Now he said this about the Spirit, which believers in him were about to receive; for as yet there was no Spirit, because Jesus was not yet glorified" (John 7:39). Here John develops the parallelism between water and the Spirit found in the Old Testament, to the point of making them identical: the living water is a symbol of the Spirit, and Jesus, source of living water, is the source of the Spirit. For John the Word remains ineffective without the intervention of the Spirit. This is why the gift of the Spirit is necessary, that is, so that the Word really becomes salvific. John affirms, "For as yet there was no Spirit, because Jesus was not yet glorified" (John 7:39), in the sense that his full gift to believers was yet to come and the era of the Spirit had not yet arrived as it would be experienced by the Church after Easter.

The "hour" of Jesus is that of his death-resurrection, the supreme moment established by the Father for the salvation of the world, which furthermore represents the moment of his glory. At that time, according to John's Gospel, the dying Jesus "gave up his Spirit" (John 19:30), an expression which historically means to give back to the Father through death the vital breath that Christ had received. Theologically, it also means the gift of the Spirit to believers. In the fourth Gospel, the last vital breath of Jesus means not only biological death, but also the Breath of the Spirit which gives life, animating creation and every living being, including the Church represented by Mary and the disciple whom Christ loved. That Spirit, which Christ himself received from the Father, he now gives to believers in the act of his redeeming death. After the resurrection, turning to the Eleven, Christ "said to them, 'Receive the Holy Spirit'" (John 20:22). He gave them the Spirit to make them new men, capable of fulfilling the mission entrusted to them, that of bringing to each person the very life which he received from the Father (see

John 6:57) and the same love that the Father has for him. At Pentecost all this comes in a superabundant way, as witnessed by St. Peter: "This Jesus God raised up and of that all of us are witnesses. Being therefore exalted at the right hand of God, and having received from the Father the promise of the Holy Spirit, he has poured out this that you both see and hear" (Acts 2:32–33).

Now Christ, as crucified and risen, can act through others thanks to his existence in the Spirit. And the disciples in Christ can experience in their lives the power of the Paraclete. John does not call the Holy Spirit the Paraclete by accident. As is attested to by some rabbinic texts, the term indicates an "intercessor," a "defender" of people at God's tribunals. For John this is the specific task of the Spirit, who, in the battle between the Church and the world, will convict the latter (see John 16:8) of its blameworthiness and its incapacity to believe in God by continuing to make present and contemporary Christ and the offer of communion with God.

The teaching of the Spirit, which envelops the entire earthly life of Jesus and which is the teaching that the glorified Jesus sends to believers through his Spirit, became in the early centuries the object of preaching and religious instruction. St. Basil, after recalling that in the history of salvation "everything is accomplished through the Spirit," pauses especially on Jesus and affirms: "From the beginning he was with the same flesh as the Lord, become inseparable chrism.... In consequence every act of Christ is achieved through the assistance of the Spirit. He was present when Christ underwent the temptation of the devil.... He was also inseparably present when Christ performed the miracles.... After the resurrection, the Spirit never again abandoned Christ. In fact, to renew humanity and return to it the grace of the breath God, which had been lost, he blew on the faces of the disciples. And what did he say? 'Receive the Holy Spirit. For those whose sins you forgive, they are forgiven; for those whose sins you retain, they are retained' (John 20:22–23)" (*On the Holy Spirit*, XVI). St. Gregory Nazianzus affirms more simply: "Christ is born and the Spirit precedes him. Christ is baptized and the Spirit gives witness. Christ is tested and the Spirit returns him to Galilee. Christ performs miracles and the Spirit accompanies him. Christ ascends to heaven and the Spirit follows him" (*Orations*, XXXI, 29).

In brief, the ultimate goal of the incarnation, besides the glorification of the Father, consists in communicating the Spirit to human beings: "Christ has rescued us from maledictions...so that in him we should receive the promise of the Spirit through faith" (see Gal. 3:13–14). This is echoed in lapidary fashion by St. Athanasius (d. 373): "The Word became flesh so that we would be able to receive the Holy Spirit. God became a wearer of the flesh so man could become a wearer of the Spirit" (*On the Incarnation of the Word*, 8). Simeon the New Theologian said: "This is the aim and the destination of every work for our salvation done by Christ: that believers receive the Holy Spirit" (*Catecheses*, VI). Nicholas Cabasilas (d. ca. 1397), another late Byzantine mystic, asks: "What in fact is the aim of Christ's sufferings, teachings, and actions? Considered in relationship to us, it is none other than the descent of the Holy Spirit on the Church" (*Commentary on the Divine Liturgy*, 37). This is why the Fathers can call Christ the great *Precursor of the Spirit*. Jesus himself said to his disciples: "It is to your advantage that I go away, for if I do not go away the Advocate will not come to you; but if I go, I will send him to you" (John 16:7). Thus, the ascension of Christ can be considered as the highest degree of *epiclesis* ("invocation," or intercession of the Father so that he might send the Spirit). In response to the invocation of the Son, the Father sends the Spirit at Pentecost and continues sending him to form the body of Christ which is the Church. "Because the Holy Spirit is the anointing of Christ, it is Christ who, as the head of the body, pours out the Spirit among his members to nourish, heal, and organize them in their mutual functions, to give them life, send them to bear witness, and associate them to his self-offering to the Father and to his intercession for the whole world. Through the Church's sacraments, Christ communicates his Holy and sanctifying Spirit to the members of his body" (CCC, 739).

Conclusion

In celebrating the two thousandth anniversary of Christian redemption we should never forget the following reality: "The redemption is totally carried out by the Son as the Anointed One, who came and acted in the power of the Holy Spirit, offering himself finally in sacrifice on the wood of the cross. And this redemption is, at the same time, constantly carried out in human hearts and minds — in the history of the world — by the Holy Spirit, who is the 'other Counselor'" (*DeV*, 24).

If the Great Jubilee is to recall the entire mystery of Christ, it is necessary to recover in full, and above all, the meaning of the *resurrection*. The Holy Spirit *today* makes present the risen Christ and communicates *life in the risen Christ*. Certainly, the Spirit reveals the "folly of the cross" (see 1 Cor. 2:6–16). But this is not an end in itself because it reveals the immense love of God and the meaning of the Gospel as the announcement of the salvation accomplished by the crucified Christ. It is necessary, in other words, to pluck the heart of the Gospel, the different logic of God which goes against that of humanity. It is the evangelical logic offered by Christ according to which life is born from death, we reign by serving, we become free and happy in the measure to which we are capable of self-giving to others without calculating and measuring the benefits. The resurrection indicates that Christian hope is not based on just any future but on faithfulness to God, characterized by definitive Love. Believing that love has no end (see 1 Cor. 13:8), Christians find hope in history open to the new covenant, walking in freedom from death and sin that imprisons human hope. The new being in Christ is expressed in justice, peace, and life. Death no longer has power because the Spirit of Christ entered definitively into the heart of history.

The Spirit works in believers in the same way that he totally penetrated the earthly and eschatological existence of Christ. Believers are "Christians" insofar as they participate in the "anointing" of Jesus, that is, in the Holy Spirit. Believers are baptized and filled with the Spirit, who transforms them into Christ. Thus, the believer's life in Christ is possible only because, and to the extent that, it is life in the Spirit. "Communion with Christ is the Holy Spirit," affirms St. Irenaeus (*Against Heresies,* III, 24, 1). This shows the need to live "in the Spirit" so as to be able to become Christlike. Only the living Spirit in the hearts of people can reveal Christ. We can say, therefore, that we become witnesses to Christ to the extent that we are "filled with the Spirit" and are his vessel. We can become the image of God in Christ only in the Spirit. As Christ is the image of the Father, so the Spirit is the image of the Son. So in having the Spirit we also have the Son. "The communion of the Spirit gives man the grace to be formed according to the fullness of the image of divine nature," said Cyril of Alexandria (*Treasury of the Trinity,* 13). "He who receives the image of the Son, that is, the Spirit, by that very fact possesses the fullness of the Father and the Son in him" (ibid.).

Chapter 5

The Holy Spirit and the Church

"Where there is the Church there is also the Spirit of God; and where there is the Spirit of God there is also the Church and every grace," affirms St. Irenaeus. He explains the reason: "The gift of God has been confided to the Church, as breath to the molded creature, so that all its members, participating in it, are given life. In it has been placed communion with Christ, that is, the Holy Spirit, guarantee of incorruptibility, confirmer of our faith, and the ladder of our ascent to God" (*Against Heresies,* III, 24, 1).

The relationship between the Spirit and the Church, as that between the Spirit and Christ, is not of the external kind nor is it an "aiding" of the Church. It is an essential relationship that constitutes the Church. "The Church has been built by the Holy Spirit," affirms St. Ambrose (*On the Holy Spirit,* II, 110). The Church insofar as it is the body of Christ, that is, the many who become *one sole* body, is the work of the Holy Spirit. It is, in fact, the mystery of the unity between the "one" (Christ) and the "many" (the believers, its members), and this unity *is* the Church. Thus the work of the Spirit is to build the Church in unity. The Church is the *mystery of communion* in the power of the *Spirit of communion.* For the Spirit, constituting the Church is dynamic, not static. It personally involves every member of the Church so that the Church is continually becoming — through the word, the sacraments, the charisms and the ministries, and, above all, through charity.

To meditate on the mystery of the Church, starting with its profound pneumatological reality, it is opportune to examine the so-called *marks,* or *attributes, of the Church* professed in the Creed: "I believe in one, holy, Catholic and apostolic Church." It is certainly the one and triune God, Father, Son, and Holy Spirit, that establishes and makes true the attributes of the Church. But every divine person has a relationship with each of these attributes. Here we will give special consideration to the action of the Spirit in the Church.

The Church Is One in Virtue of the Spirit

"One Lord, one faith, one baptism" (Eph. 4:4), writes St. Paul. The Second Vatican Council affirms: "It is the Holy Spirit, dwelling in those who believe and pervading and ruling over the entire Church, who brings about that wonderful communion of the faithful and joins them together so intimately in Christ that he is the principle of the Church's unity" (*UR,* 2).

As previously emphasized, the essence of the Church is its *mystery of communion* because it is the sacrament and icon of the Trinity. According to the well-known definition of St. Cyprian, it is "a people brought *into unity* from the unity of the Father, the Son, and the Holy Spirit" (*On the Lord's Prayer,* 23; see *LG,* 4). Around the year 200 the North African ecclesiastical author Tertullian wrote: "Wherever the three — the Father, Son, and Holy Spirit — are, there is the Church, the body of the three" (*On Baptism,* 6). As the Spirit is the link of union and communion between the Father and the Son in the intimate and eternal existence of the Trinity, so in the Church he is the ineffable gift of the Father which unites all the baptized in one body, the body of Christ. "Because we all have received the same and unique spirit," said Cyril of Alexandria, "that is, the Holy Spirit, we are all mixed together, so to say, one with the other and with God.

Even if we are multiple and separate and even if in each of us Christ puts the Spirit of the Father and his own, this Spirit is one and indivisible. In this way Christ, by himself, reduces to unity the spirits of the individual persons and makes them all appear as one thing in him. The power of the holy humanity of Christ makes those in whom he is found share his body. In the same way the unique and indivisible Spirit of God which lives in us leads everyone to spiritual unity," (*Commentary on the Gospel of John,* XII, 11). The following is sung in the Byzantine Pentecost liturgy: the Holy Spirit is he who "holds together the entire institution of the Church."

The Spirit is, therefore, the principle of communion because the *Agape* (Love) unites by its nature. "God's love has been poured into our hearts through the Holy Spirit that has been given to us" (Rom. 5:5; see CCC, 737). He is the principle of unity and communion because the unity of the Church is a grace and gift of God. This grace is constantly given to each person as it is constantly given to life and existence. The unity of the Church is an eminent grace that God gives to us; it is offered in communion with him and with our brothers and sisters. This unity is a participation in the life of God which becomes activated with our incorporation to Christ. Becoming *one with Christ,* we build the Church, fulfilling the eternal design of God. Jesus became incarnate, died, and rose again so that this unity could be accomplished to return human beings, injured by sin, to unity with the Father, Son, and Holy Spirit (see Eph. 2:11). For this unity, Jesus prayed during his passion that "all may be one" as he and the Father are one (see John 17:11, 21). In the current plan of salvation no grace is given to people except in the Spirit. This is especially true for the highest degree of grace, that of the union between Christ the head and his members, that is, the body of Christ which is the Church. "The faithful are one because, in the Spirit, they are in communion with the Son and, in him, share in his communion with the Father.... For the Catholic Church, then, the communion of Christians is none other than the manifestation in them of the grace by which God makes them sharers in his own communion, which is his eternal life" (*UUS*, 9).

The Holy Spirit is the one who accomplishes unity in communion, not only of the individual faithful in relation to the whole, but also in the individual Churches in relationship to the one Church. Here we see the importance of the collegial character of the Church (see *CCC*, 879), which springs from the founding experience of the apostles. Christ constituted these apostles "in the form of a college or permanent assembly, at the head of which he placed Peter, chosen from amongst them" (*LG*, 19). It is in communion with the pope, bishop of Rome and successor to St. Peter, and with the college of bishops, expression of unity and diversity in the Church, that every local Church, "a portion of the people of God," finds its constitutive identity. This is how, thanks to the Eucharist, every local Church is fully Church and is one Church, a Church in communion with the others which profess the same Eucharist.

The Spirit is also at work to accomplish the perfect unity of the Church. The Second Vatican Council affirms this regarding the various non-Catholic Churches and Christian communities and the Catholic Church. "These Christians are indeed in some real way joined to us in the Holy Spirit for, by his gifts and graces, his sanctifying power is also active in them and he has strengthened some of them even to the shedding of their blood. And so the Spirit stirs up desires and actions in all of Christ's disciples in order that all may be peaceably united, as Christ ordained, in one flock under one shepherd" (*LG*, 15).

In this way the Spirit achieves not only the unity of the Church but also its *diversity*, granting a variety of *charisms*

and gifts to individual faithful as well as to local Churches
(see *LG*, 13), without harming unity (see 1 Cor. 12:4–11).
It even enriches unity because first among the charisms is
charity (see 1 Cor. 13:13). "What a stupendous mystery!"
exclaimed Clement of Alexandria (d. ca. 220). "There is
only one Father of the universe, only one Logos of the universe, and also only one Holy Spirit everywhere. There is
also only one virgin, and I love to call her the Church"
(*Paedagogus*, I, 6).

The Church Is Holy in Virtue of the Sanctifying Spirit

St. Basil said: "There is no holiness without the Holy Spirit"
(*On the Holy Spirit*, XVI, 38). This expression applies first of
all to the entire Church as such and then, to all its members.

The unity of the triune communion constitutes the *holiness* of the Church. It is "holy" because it *participates* in
the trinitarian nature of the "total otherness" of God "three
times holy," and especially in the holiness of the Spirit,
called "Holy" because he is considered to be God's actual
indwelling. We must make clear that we are not speaking
primarily of a *moral* holiness, but of a holiness which regards *being*. "The Holy Spirit is truly holy because nothing
is holy to this degree and in this manner. It is not acquired
holiness, but holiness in person," said Gregory of Nazianzus
(*Orations*, XXV, 16). The Spirit is, in fact, the "communion"
between the Father and the Son, between Christ and humanity — the unity which constitutes the Church — and between
the Church and the Father, so that "through him both of us
have access in one Spirit to the Father" (Eph. 2:18). In the
final analysis we can affirm that in the economy of salvation
the holy nature of God is communicated to human beings
by the Holy Spirit. This is what forms the holiness of the
Church. "The union of God with men is accomplished by

work of the Holy Spirit," affirms St. John Damascene (*Sermon for the Feast of the Nativity of the Theotokos,* 3). As the Spirit sanctified the humanity of Christ, so he continues to sanctify his mystical body, the Church, said Cyril of Alexandria (*Commentary on the Gospel of John,* XI, 11). The same Doctor of the Church affirms that because the Spirit is "holy by nature, sanctification belongs to him" (*On the Trinity,* VI).

Especially evocative are some of the images which biblical revelation and Christian tradition have used to indicate the holiness of the Church as produced by the Spirit.

The New Testament speaks of the holiness of the Church, calling it the holy temple of God (see 1 Cor. 3:16ff.; Eph. 2:21), whose faithful "like living stones, let yourselves be built into a spiritual house, to be a holy priesthood" (1 Pet. 2:5). The *Church is temple,* an assembly of faithful, holy people assembled and sanctified by the Spirit. "The Church of Christ is holy. The temple of God is holy and this temple is you (see 1 Cor. 3:17). From this comes the expression *sanctam ecclesiam*" (Thomas Aquinas, *Commentary on "I Believe in God,"* art. IX). This is the holy temple of God in which, by virtue of the living water which is the Spirit, faith is celebrated in Baptism and in the Eucharist. "Temple" and "house" allude to the idea of habitation. The New Testament speaks of the indwelling of the Three in the soul. It refers not only to the Father and the Son, but expressly to the Spirit (see John 14:15–17; 1 Cor. 3:16–17). "No one has ever seen God; if we love one another, God lives in us, and his love is perfected in us. By this we know that we abide in him and he in us, because he has given us of his Spirit" (1 John 4:12–13). This does not refer to an exterior dwelling of the Spirit but to a presence which touches the essence of the person and transforms him, transfiguring him and "consecrating him." The indwelling of the Spirit in the soul derives from the original and primary reality of the dwelling of the Spirit in the body of Christ, which is the Church. Just as in the baptism of Christ, the Spirit "sanctified" and "consecrated" Christ's body of flesh, so at Pentecost did he sanctify and consecrate Christ's "mystical" body, the Church.

The ontological holiness of the Church — communion with the Trinity — is then accomplished through the communion of the *holy things,* that is, the sacraments, the Word, and the charisms. All this takes place so that the Church is a *communion of saints* as is recited in the Creed. The letter to the Ephesians expresses this truth: "For through him [Christ] both of us have access in one Spirit to the Father. So then you are no longer strangers and aliens, but you are citizens with the saints and also members of the household of God, built upon the foundation of the apostles and the prophets, with Christ Jesus himself as the cornerstone. In him the whole structure is joined together and grows into a holy temple of the Lord; in whom you also are built together spiritually into the dwelling place of God" (Eph. 2:18–22).

Here is seen the action of the Holy Spirit, who exercises a continuing discernment in the "need of purification" (*LG,* 8), which connotes the road of the conversion of the Church. In this sense, even the moral holiness of innumerable sons and daughters of the Church is due to the direct action of the Holy Spirit, as the Fathers of the Church affirm: "Since Pentecost the Church is full of saints." "The Holy One who sanctifies, helps, and teaches the Church is, in fact, the Holy Spirit, the Paraclete" (Cyril of Jerusalem, *Catecheses,* XVI, 14). He has come down from heaven "to defend and sanctify the Church, as a guide for souls and a helmsman for storm-tossed humankind, a light to guide the wayfarers, a judge who presides over the contest and the crowning of the victorious" (*Catecheses,* XVII, 13).

Furthermore, the Church is a *communio sanctorum* (communion of saints), but this does not mean it is free of sinners. Sin in the Church is precisely the refusal to be *in communion in the Spirit*. The ancient monks, for this reason, called a holy Christian a *pneumatophoros*, that is, a bearer of the Spirit, while a person living in sin was "empty of the Spirit." The task of the Church is to progressively lead its members to live in holiness, which consists of communion with the Father through the Son in the Holy Spirit. Only in this way can the Church be the sacrament and icon of trinitarian communion and, thus, a "sign raised in the midst of the nations."

The Church Is Catholic in the Fullness of the Spirit

The word "catholic" derives from the Greek words *kata* and *holos* — "according to" and "whole" — and means "universal" in the sense of "according to, in keeping with the whole." The word indicates that the catholicity of the Church expresses above all a dimension of *qualitative* fullness, a vertical dimension. Only secondly does it indicate a dimension of *quantitative* fullness, a horizontal, extensive one. The latter is a secondary expression derived from the first. The fullness of the Church is linked to the fullness of Christ, insofar as it is his body (see *CCC*, 830).

Once again, the Holy Spirit is at the roots of the meaning of catholicity. The *Catechism* says: "The Church was, in this fundamental sense, catholic on the day of Pentecost and will always be so until the day of the Parousia" (*CCC*, 830). This "fullness-catholicity" of interiorizing and penetration, due to the joint and reciprocal action of the Spirit and of Christ, extends to all the faithful and to every local Church (see *LG*, 23). This fullness, fruit of Easter and Pentecost, acts so that the local Church is truly in the universal Church.

The Holy Spirit assures not only the internal catholicity of the Church but also the extensive understanding, reuniting in one body people different by sex, race, and nationality. A very beautiful text by Maximus the Confessor attests to this: "Men, women, children profoundly different regarding race, nationality, language, social class, work, knowledge, dignity, goods...are all sought by the Church in the Spirit. He equally stamps a divine form on all. All persons receive from him a unique nature impossible to break, a nature which no longer permits the taking account of the multiple and profound differences which are theirs. From this derives the fact that we are all united in a truly Catholic manner. No one is separated from the community in the Church. The foundation for one and all is the indivisible strength of the faith. Christ is all in everyone. He assumes all to himself according to his infinite strength, and he communicates his goodness to all. He is like a center where all lines converge. The creatures of the one God are no longer strangers and enemies one to the other for lack of a common place where they can show their friendship and peace" (*Mystagogia,* I). Thus, the Church, thanks to the Holy Spirit, is the place where truly the assembly of peoples, of all peoples, become family, a holy people united in faith, love, and peace!

The Church, as a consequence, cannot be closed unto itself, separated from the world, imprisoning the Spirit within its limits. If this were the case, the action of the Spirit would be limited. On the contrary, the Spirit uses his *mission* to open the Church toward the world. "The Holy Spirit is indeed the principal agent of the whole of the Church's mission" (*RM,* 21).

The Church Is Apostolic through the Perpetual Sending of the Spirit

By the action of the Holy Spirit, the Church is apostolic. It is the historical dimension of the triune communion and visible reality of the communion with the apostles. Believing in the apostolic *Church* means believing the Spirit who made the *Church* apostolic. On Pentecost the Spirit descended on the apostles and those gathered around them. From that first nucleus the Church has multiplied until today.

This communion with the apostles implies the fidelity of the Church to the doctrine revealed by Jesus and transmitted by the apostles: "When the time for Jesus to leave this world had almost come, he told the apostles of 'another counselor....' A little while after the prediction just mentioned, Jesus adds: 'But the Counselor, the Holy Spirit, whom the Father will send in my name, he will teach you all things, and bring to your remembrance all that I have said to you.' The Holy Spirit will be the counselor of the apostles and the Church, always present in their midst — even though invisible — as the teacher of the same good news that Christ proclaimed. The words 'he will teach' and 'bring to remembrance' mean only that he, in his own particular way, will continue to inspire the spreading of the Gospel of salvation, but also that he will help people to understand the correct meaning of the context of Christ's message; they mean that he will ensure continuity and unity of understanding in the midst of changing conditions and circumstances. The Holy Spirit, then, will ensure that in the Church there will always continue the same truth which the apostles heard from their master" (*DeV*, 3–4).

The task of the Spirit to ensure the Church's permanence in truth has at least two aspects. The first is to remind the Church of its original vocation and source: the revelation of

Christ, in which the Gospel constitutes the perennial newness of Christianity. To remember the teaching of the apostles
means to belong to the school of that tradition which "makes
progress in the Church, with the help of the Holy Spirit"
(*DV,* 8). The second aspect is recalling the eschatological
dimension of the Church. In fidelity to the *kerygma,* the
Church is the beginning of the kingdom, always on the move
to accomplish peace, freedom, and justice. Pentecost, therefore, perpetuates through the centuries the presence of Jesus
among us and also his teaching transmitted by the apostles
and their successors, and which is that believed by the people
of God. The Spirit is the one who brings to life this teaching. He prevents it from being reduced to simple and abstract
enunciations of truth and makes it "spirit and life," revealing
the face of Christ, image of the Father.

In this larger sense, *the entire Church is apostolic.* Individual believers are also apostolic since they possess and live the
truth transmitted by the apostles.

Finally, the Church is apostolic by the strength of *apostolic succession.* On Pentecost, in fact, the apostles felt full of
strength. "It is precisely this that the Holy Spirit worked in
them, and this is continually at work in the Church, though
their successors. For the grace of the Holy Spirit, which the
apostles gave to their collaborators through the imposition
of hands, continues to be transmitted in episcopal ordina-
tion. The bishops, in turn, by the sacrament of orders renders
the sacred ministers sharers in this spiritual gift and, through
the sacrament of Confirmation, ensure that all who are reborn of water and the Holy Spirit are strengthened by this
gift. And thus, in a certain way, the grace of Pentecost is
perpetuated in the Church" (*DeV,* 25).

From what has been said, it is understood that the Church
is "built upon the foundation of the apostles" (Eph. 2:20;
see 1 Pet. 2:5; Rev. 21:14). It is apostolic not only because

of the truth transmitted but also by the fact that the charism of the apostles lives and works in their successors, the bishops in communion with the successor of Peter. "By virtue of the Holy Spirit, Peter, head of the apostles and guardian of the keys to the kingdom of heaven, also acts" (Cyril of Jerusalem, *Catecheses*, XVII, 27).

From this perspective, the action of the Spirit in the Church does not exclude the institutional dimension but presupposes and reinforces it. The bishops, with the bishop of Rome the first among them, exercise the charism of teaching, guiding, and sanctifying the people of God, thus building the body of Christ, which is the Church (see *UUS*, 88). As has been noted, every charism is a gift of the Spirit in the Church and for the Church. "There is only one Spirit who, according to his own richness and the needs of the ministries, gives his different gifts for the welfare of the Church (see 1 Cor. 12:1–11). Among these gifts the primacy belongs to the grace of the apostles to whose authority the Spirit himself subjects even those who are endowed with charisms" (*LG*, 7). With this in mind, St. Basil asks: "Is not Church order clearly and without a doubt the work of the Spirit?...This order is according to the gifts of the Spirit" (*On the Holy Spirit*, XVI, 39).

The bishops, for their part, have the charism of *keeping watch* so that in every Church unity is realized, along with the Church's other marks, or characteristics, exercising this charism in union with the bishop of Rome. "The mission of the bishop of Rome within the college of all the pastors consists precisely in 'keeping watch' (*episkopein*) [from which the word *episkopos*, or bishop, is derived], like a sentinel, so that through the efforts of the pastors the true voice of Christ the shepherd may be heard in all the particular Churches entrusted to those pastors, the *una, sancta, catholica et apostolica ecclesia* is made present" (*UUS*, 94).

The ways in which the Spirit bestows apostolicity on the Church, besides through the successors of the apostles, are many. First of all, the charism of the bishops is not given through a simple juridical act but through a sacrament, the sacrament of apostolicity, that is, the episcopate. This is communicated to the bishops by the imposition of hands and by the invocation of the Holy Spirit (see *LG*, 21).

In the second place, the bishops and their priests build the Church with the *eucharistic celebration,* which is the "summit toward which the activity of the Church is directed; it is also the fount from which her power flows" (*SC*, 10). This is done because — as we will see below — the Eucharist, and liturgical action in general, does not occur without the Holy Spirit. He makes real in the present for our salvation the mystery of Christ performed in the past.

Still more, the bishops nourish the Church with the Word and the *kerygma* (announcement of the "good news") of the apostles. This *fidelity* in transmitting, developing, interiorizing, and actualizing the apostolic tradition is the work of the Spirit (see *DV,* 8; *LG,* 25).

The Church Spreads by Evangelizing in the Spirit

From the overview just presented, we see that the Holy Spirit makes the Word of God, in its various phases, a part of history. The Spirit inspires Scripture, speaks through the prophets, accomplishes the becoming human of the Word given in its fullness in Christ, and fills the Church, the body of Christ. Even today the Word of God is given to humanity by the Church through his work, especially evangelization, in obedience to the command of the Lord: "Go therefore and make disciples of all nations" (Matt. 28:19). Only by having the Spirit of the Lord forever as protagonist can the Church, "one, holy, catholic, and apostolic," be spread among people. The words of Peter's first letter can be applied to the Christians of every era: "It was revealed to them that they were serving not themselves but you, in regard to the things that have now been announced to you through those who brought you good news by the Holy Spirit sent from heaven" (1 Pet. 1:12).

The Evangelizing Vocation of the Church

In the design of the triune God's revelation, the Church is a "sacrament — a sign and instrument, that is, of communion with God and of unity among all men" (*LG*, 1). It is in the Church that humanity can search for and discover the true God, and it is through the Church that God's plan of love can be known by every human being. The task of the Church, therefore, is to make the call of God echo in every person, the God who is "for us and for our salvation." This is the meaning of evangelization: "Evangelization is in fact the grace and vocation proper to the Church, her deepest identity. She exists in order to evangelize, that is to say in order to preach and teach, to be the channel of the gift of grace" (*EN*, 14).

Furthermore, "On the threshold of the new millennium Christians need to place themselves humbly before the Lord and examine themselves on the responsibility which they too have for the evils of our day. The present age in fact, together with much light, also presents not a few shadows.

"How can we remain silent, for example, about the religious indifference which causes many people today to live as if God did not exist or to be content with a vague religiosity, incapable of coming to grips with the question of truth and the requirement of consistency? To this must also be added the widespread loss of the transcendent sense of human life and confusion in the ethical sphere, even about the fundamental values of respect for life and the family. The sons and daughters of the Church, too, need to examine themselves in this regard. To what extent have they been shaped by the climate of secularism and ethical relativism? And what responsibility do they bear, in view of the increasing lack of religion, for having 'failed in their religious, moral, or social life'?" (*TMA*, 36).

"He Is the Principal Agent of Mission" (RM, 30)

The Church *must* evangelize and even reevangelize a world which is often de-Christianized and secularized. "Evangelization," however, "will never be possible without the action of the Holy Spirit," affirms Paul VI (*EN*, 75). John Paul II, adopting the teaching of his predecessor, presses the point: "In our own day too, the Spirit is the principal agent of the new evangelization. Hence it will be important to gain a renewed appreciation of the Spirit as the one who builds the kingdom of God within the course of history and prepares its full manifestation in Jesus Christ, stirring people's hearts and quickening in our world the seeds of the full salvation which will come at the end of time" (*TMA*, 45).

Without the intervention of the Spirit, all Church preaching and religious instruction would certainly be ineffective because only the Holy Spirit can stir in the hearts of people and society the hope of salvation. "The techniques of evangelization are good, but even the most advanced ones could not replace the gentle action of the Spirit. The most perfect preparation of the evangelizer has no effect without the Holy Spirit. Without the Holy Spirit the most convincing dialectic has no power over the heart of man. Without him the most highly developed schemas resting on a sociological or psychological basis are quickly seen to be quite valueless. ... Now if the Spirit of God has a preeminent place in the whole life of the Church, it is in her evangelizing mission that he is most active. It is not by chance that the great inauguration of evangelization took place on the morning of Pentecost, under the inspiration of the Spirit" (*EN*, 75).

Jesus and the Apostles Evangelize in the Power of the Spirit

The evangelizing mission of Jesus is presented in the synoptic Gospels, especially in Luke, as the work of the Holy Spirit. After the temptation in the desert "Jesus, filled with the power of the Spirit, returned to Galilee....He began to teach in their synagogues" (Luke 4:4–14). In the long citation of Isaiah 61:1–2, with which Jesus inaugurates his preaching in Nazareth, it can be seen how all his evangelical work is put under the action of the Spirit.

Acts 2:1–41, in turn, makes evident how apostolic preaching became effective only after the apostles received the Holy Spirit. The text, which presents the first Pentecostal experience of the Church, signals the paradigmatic itinerary of every positive reception of the faith. Peter, beginning to speak under inspiration (Acts 2:14), affirms that the event is the fulfillment of the Old Testament promise regarding the eschatological gift of the Spirit (Acts 2:15–21). He then continues, announcing the *kerygma* (Acts 2:22–36) concerning Jesus as "messiah" and "Lord" (Acts 2:36), the author of the gift of the Spirit (Acts 2:33). Peter closes with an appeal to conversion and Baptism to obtain forgiveness from sins and the gift of the Spirit (Acts 2:38–40). Finally, he emphasizes the positive reception of the Word by the listeners (Acts 2:41).

Only a "Spiritualized" Apostle Can Effectively Evangelize

The Spirit wants the cooperation of humanity so that the Gospel can "take root" through "spiritual" people. This is why evangelization requires being disposed to the action of the Spirit. Paul VI affirms: "The Church is an evangelizer, but she begins by being evangelized herself. She is the community of believers, the community of hope lived and communicated, the community of brotherly love; and she needs to listen unceasingly to what she must believe, to her reasons for hoping, to the new commandment of love" (*EN*, 15). Let us evoke the image of the crystal which radiates from every side the light of the sun. St. Basil uses it when he wants to say that the soul must be "clear" to be able to reflect the light of the Spirit and the truth of the faith. "As very transparent and clear bodies, on contact with a light beam, also become luminous and emit new rays, so do souls which have in them the Spirit. They are illuminated by the Spirit and also become holy and reflect grace to others" (*On the Holy Spirit*, IX, 23). Evangelization does not mean announcing abstract truth but the Truth, the person of Christ with whom people are invited to come into communion. It is the Spirit alone who can allow this to happen until the wedding union. The evangelizer is thus called to collaborate with the Spirit so that this miracle can take place. The more receptive the evangelizer's collaboration is with the Paraclete, the more effective will be the evangelization. "The apostles did not come down from the mountain like Moses, their hands holding stone tablets. They left the Upper Room carrying the Holy Spirit in their hearts and offering to everyone the treasures of wisdom, grace, and spiritual gifts as if they were coming from a gushing spring. They went, in fact, to preach to the whole world as if they were the very living law, and as if free because animated by the grace of the Holy Spirit" (St. John Chrysostom, *Homily on the Gospel of Matthew*, I).

On the other hand, evangelization has the aim of creating communities: "The Spirit leads the company of believers to 'form a community,' to be the Church. After Peter's first proclamation on the day of Pentecost and the conversations that followed, the first communities take shape (see Acts 2:42–47; 4:32–35). "One of the central purposes of mission is to bring people together in hearing the Gospel, in fraternal communion, in prayer and in the Eucharist" (*RM*, 26).

Conclusion

Given these considerations, we can say that the Great Jubilee becomes a unique occasion to rediscover the mystery of the Church, emphasizing in the light of the Spirit its evangelizing vocation in announcing the Gospel to the world. In this, the role of the Spirit in the building of the Church becomes evident. "Because the Spirit is communion with the Father and with the Son, they have wished for us to have communion among ourselves and with them in the Holy Spirit, who is God and the gift of God. . . . It is in him that the people of God are joined in unity. . . . The Church is the very work of the Holy Spirit and outside of him there is no remission of sins" (St. Augustine, *Sermons*, LXXI). Rediscovering the role of the Holy Spirit means involving every believer in the new Pentecost that the Jubilee can represent, above all in rediscovering the true role of the Church, sacrament of Christ's presence in history.

The principal work of the Spirit, who is the Spirit of "communion," consists in rendering the Church ever more a sign of God's trinitarian love. The Spirit makes every member of the Church a being-in-relationship, whose identity is expressed in the logic of communion and solidarity. If believers want to be genuine, they can only become Church and live communion as a style of evangelization, experiencing the unity whose source is the Spirit. "To believe in Christ means to desire unity; to desire unity means to desire the Church; to desire the Church means to desire the communion of grace which corresponds to the Father's plan for all eternity" (*UUS*, 9).

Thus, the mission of the Church in today's reality is to be the sign and ferment of universality. This mission must be accomplished, above all, in an atmosphere of contemporary religious pluralism, which subverts and seems to unhook religious experience from any historical mediation, in an atmosphere marked by the relativizing of doctrinal formulations. It will be opportune to rediscover the roots of Catholic identity in the awareness that the Gospel is for every person, just as the Church is for all in the strength of the Spirit — the link of unity between God and the world. The Church, because it is communion and unity in diversity, is the universal sign of salvation, a messianic people in dialogue between Christianity and society and between Christianity and religions.

In second place is the incessant commitment to Christian unity in the one truth of Jesus Christ. The pope affirms: "At the dawn of the new millennium, how can we not implore from the Lord, with renewed enthusiasm and a deeper awareness, the grace to prepare ourselves, together, to offer this sacrifice of unity?" (*UUS*, 102). He also recommends this in *Tertio Millennio Adveniente*: "The reflection of the faithful in the second year of preparation ought to focus particularly on the value of unity within the Church, to which the various gifts and charisms bestowed upon her by the Spirit are directed. In this regard, it will be opportune to promote a deeper understanding of the ecclesiological doctrine of the Second Vatican Council as contained primarily in the dogmatic constitution *Lumen Gentium*. This important document has expressly emphasized that the unity of the body of Christ is founded on the activity of the Holy Spirit, guaranteed by the apostolic ministry and sustained by mutual love (see 1 Cor. 13:1–8). This catechetical enrichment of the faith cannot fail to bring the members of the people of God to a more mature awareness of their own responsibilities, as well as to a more lively sense of the importance of ecclesial obedience" (*TMA*, 47).

The Great Jubilee, therefore, must constitute an important moment for the full recovery of the Christian vocation of universality and unity in multiplicity, in which the Church is the prophetic sign of truth within love (see Eph. 4:15) and of reconciliation in the world. A beautiful text of St. Augustine is very suggestive. It says that having the Spirit means to be in the Church, and being in the Church means to be universal, truly "catholic" in name and in fact: "The Church itself speaks the languages of all peoples. First the Church was enclosed in one population, where it spoke the languages of all. Speaking the languages of all was a sign that in the future, growing among the people, it would speak the languages of everybody. Those who are not in this Church do not now receive the Holy Spirit. Those who are separated and detached from the unity of the members — the unity of which speaks the languages of all — become aware that they do not have him [the Spirit]. If they have him, they give the sign he gave them: they speak the languages of everybody. And (you will object to me) you perhaps speak every language? Certainly, because every language is mine, that is, in the body of which I am a member. Spread among the people, the Church speaks every language. The Church is the body of Christ. In this body you are a member. Being a member of that body that speaks every language, you also, be assured, speak all languages. The unity of the members coincides in charity, and this unity speaks as one man spoke then. We too receive the Holy Spirit if we love the Church, if we are melded into charity, if we take joy in the name catholic and in the catholic faith. Brothers and sisters, we believe that to the extent that we love the Church, to that extent we have the Holy Spirit.... Therefore, we have the Holy Spirit if we love the Church. We love it if we persevere in its body and in its charity" (*Discourse on the Gospel of John*, 32:7–8).

Chapter 6

Mary and the Spirit

Meditating on the Holy Spirit for the Great Jubilee implies taking a look at the woman who gave birth to Jesus through the Spirit. As it is impossible to conceive of Christ and the Church without the indispensable intervention of the Holy Spirit, so is it impossible to think of Mary, the mother of God, "type and outstanding model" of the Church (*LG*, 53), outside of a pneumatological context.

The profound action of the Holy Spirit in the history of salvation leads us to analyze, affirmed Paul VI, "the hidden relationship between the Spirit of God and the Virgin of Nazareth, and show the influence they exert on the Church" (*MC*, 27). This gives us special reason in preparing for the Great Jubilee to reflect on aspects of this relationship between Mary and the Spirit.

Mary, Docile Resting Place of the Spirit

Everything that Mary became with her free acceptance and her collaboration she owes to her son, Jesus, and the action of the Holy Spirit. The Virgin is the *all holy* because from the first moment of her existence she was the "temple of the Holy Spirit" (*LG*, 53). "Full of grace" means nothing other than "full of the Holy Spirit," because it is always the Spirit who brings about communion with the entire Trinity. "The Father predestined her but the sanctifying virtue of the Spirit visited her, purified her, made her holy and, so to say, immaculate," wrote St. John Damascene (*Homily on the Dormition,* I, 3). Mary's transformation by the Spirit was so profound from the beginning as to touch her very essence. Theophanes of Nicea, a Byzantine author of the fourteenth century, writes: "Mary from the beginning was united with the Spirit, author of life; everything that she experienced she shared with the Spirit so that her participation in the Spirit became a participation in being" (*Discourse on the Mother of God,* 30). This is the real reason why Mary was *all holy* from the first moment of her existence.

Mary was molded and made into a new creature by the Spirit. This "original holiness" of Mary was not something passive, however, because from the moment she became conscious of this she collaborated in a unique way with the Spirit to nurture that intense and profound union with God.

The Spirit guided Mary her entire life, especially in the most salient moments of her existence, just as he leads the children of God (see Rom. 8:14) and as he guided Jesus in the desert (see Luke 4:1).

He guided her at the time of the *Annunciation* when, sustained and inspired by the Spirit, she freely consented to become the mother of the Word, she who "responded, therefore, with all her human and feminine 'I,' and this response of faith included both perfect cooperation with 'the grace of God that precedes and assists' and perfect openness to the action of the Holy Spirit, who constantly brings faith to completion by his gifts" (*RMa,* 13). She cooperated with the Spirit in the visit to her cousin Elizabeth when, inspired by the Spirit, she "prophesied," or pronounced words inspired by the "breath" of God, interpreted the history of salvation according to the "logic" of God, and proved to be the "humble one of God" always disposed to fulfill the will of the Lord. The *Magnificat* is the inspired expression of her sentiments. This was made possible because, as Martin Luther said, she "had personal experience through the Holy Spirit who illuminated and instructed her. . . . [In this way] she learned from the Holy Spirit the great knowledge that God did not want to manifest his power in any way other than elevating that which is low and lowering that which is high" (Martin Luther, WA 7, 546).

The Spirit was not only present at the birth of Christ, helping Mary to believe that "her" baby was the fulfillment of the promise God made to the patriarchs: he who is born of her was truly "holy; he will be called Son of God" (Luke 1:35). He also accompanied Mary during the growth of Jesus, even in the most difficult and mysterious moments when she had need to "meditate" and interiorize these events so that she could become more deeply aware of their importance and significance (see Luke 2:19, 49–51).

"I am convinced that no man can exist capable of suffering as much as the Virgin suffered," affirms Nicholas Cabasilas (*Homily on the Assumption,* 11). Even at the foot of the cross Mary had need of special assistance from the Spirit. She did not leave when faced with the harshness of the death of the Son, but pronounced her yes in the Spirit and became the mother of those for whom Christ offered his life.

In the Upper Room, afterward, Mary — as if in a great *epiclesis* — invokes the Father with her supplications until he sends his Spirit: "But since it had pleased God not to manifest solemnly the mystery of the salvation of the human race before he would pour forth the Spirit promised by Christ, we see the apostles before the day of Pentecost 'preserving with one mind in prayer with the women and Mary the Mother of Jesus, and with his brethren' (Acts 1:14), and we also see Mary by her prayers imploring the gift of the Spirit, who had already overshadowed her in the Annunciation" (*LG,* 59).

The Virgin, completely penetrated and transformed by the Spirit, is "vivified" by him and "redeemed" even from corporal decay and "assumed" into heaven. The Byzantine theologian Nicholas Cabasilas affirms that by her sublime holiness and the radical transformation undergone by the presence of the Spirit, Mary had already, during her life, a "spiritualized body, that is, one transformed by the Spirit." She was so completely penetrated by him "who is the Lord and gives life" that she already possessed the source of immortal life. The Virgin possessed that life "in the Spirit" while she lived on earth, but it was hidden. However, when her earthly life came to a close, she radiated immortality in the same way as it shone from Christ after his death (see Nicholas Cabasilas, *Homily on the Assumption*, 10–11). Mary's assumption into heaven was nothing but the full effect of her "spiritualization."

Some aspects of this relationship between Mary and the Spirit need to be deepened because they regard in a special way the "anamnesis" of the Great Jubilee.

Mary in Virtue of the Spirit Becomes Mother of God

All the greatness of Mary consists in the fact that she is the "Mother of God." This is the central point of all that the Virgin is in herself and in her relationship to believers. The Spirit is present and effective in a most precise way in this divine maternity, as this is the work of the Holy Spirit. We are indebted to the Spirit for that event, which took place two thousand years ago, and which the Church prepares to celebrate in the Great Jubilee. It is opportune to pause and meditate on *how* Mary *virginally* becomes the Mother of God.

The Holy Spirit, in the present economy of salvation, is always the *precursor of Christ*. Without the previous descent and activity of the Spirit, there can be no visible presence of the Word.

The *Annunciation to the Virgin* is the most evident and

most important event in this process of the divine economy. This salvific fact in which "our salvation began" already represents a pentecost. The Spirit descends on Mary in an effective way to make the Son of God a human being. Mary asked, "How can this come about?" In other words, how can I virginally conceive a baby? The angel responded: "The Holy Spirit will come upon you, and the power of the Most High will overshadow you" (Luke 1:35). The Creed professes that Jesus was "born of the Virgin Mary by the work of the Holy Spirit." The Holy Spirit who descends on Mary and surrounds her is "he who gives life." It is he who from the beginning of time has progressively made known in history the Word of God. And, now, in the fullness of time, the Son of God, through the Spirit's power, is made man in the womb of the Virgin. The Fathers of the Church affirm: "When Mary gave her answer to God, she received the Spirit, who molded in her that flesh equal to God."

Why, we may ask, does this "becoming flesh" of the Word, his becoming man, take place in the very womb of Mary, the Virgin of Nazareth? Why has such an involvement between a human creature and the Holy Spirit never happened in any other moment of human history? In Mary all this took place with the minimum of resistance. We read in *Lumen Gentium*, no. 56: "It is no wonder then that it was customary for the Fathers to refer to the Mother of God as all holy and free from every stain of sin, as though fashioned by the Holy Spirit and formed as a new creature." Thus did the Spirit, through her and in her, without any resistance render the Word fully present. Through the Spirit the Word was "introduced into history." The Spirit united the visible to the invisible and thus fulfilled the eternal design of God to "recapitulate all things in Christ." The ancient tradition of the Church affirms that God the Father, making of Mary a "vessel of the Spirit" and his depository, renders Mary's womb "fertile," and thus "the ineffable triumph of the virginal conception takes place" (from the Canon of Andrew of Crete). By reason of Mary's total "spiritualization," she could offer the gift of Christ. She who was "full of grace," that is, the Spirit, in her total capacity to receive the Spirit can communicate divine life in the Spirit.

As can be surmised, the relationship of Mary with the Holy Spirit possesses such a special intensity that in Christian tradition it is expressed in the title "Mary, bride of the Holy Spirit." This expression was especially dear to St. Francis of Assisi, who prayed to the Virgin in this manner: "Holy Virgin Mary, there is no one similar to you born in the world among women, daughter and maidservant of the All High King, the heavenly Father, mother of the holiest Lord Jesus Christ, *bride of the Holy Spirit*; pray for us with St. Michael the Archangel and with all the powers of heaven, and with all the saints, to your most holy beloved Son, our Lord " (*Officium Passionis*). In his encyclical *Redemptoris Mater* John Paul II refers to Mary in the Upper Room on the day of Pentecost: "In a sense her journey of faith is longer. The Holy Spirit had already come down upon her, and she became his faithful spouse at the annunciation, welcoming the Word of the true God" (*RMa*, 26).

In this context, the expression "Mary, bride of the Holy Spirit" signifies nothing other than this mystical but fertile union between the person of Mary and the Spirit who "gives life." From this we can also understand the meaning of Mary's virginity. More than a *moral virtue*, it is a mode of being in the Spirit and of participating in the Christic fertility of the Spirit. Mary is *mother*, that is, fertile, not according to human necessity or by biological "logic," but because she has been made so by the Spirit, whose task is only to make present and visible the invisible, "to make the Word flesh." To engender Christ, Mary has no need of human intervention, for she is the living transparency of the Spirit. From him and only from him does Mary attain the force and efficacy of the fecundity of her womb. He who "creates and gives life to the universe," he from whom alone derives the reality worth calling "life," has given life to the womb of Mary and made fertile her virginity.

Thus, to initiate the earthly life of Jesus, the Spirit *had need* of the womb and free collaboration of a virgin; otherwise Jesus could not have been brother of other human beings and their savior!

Mary's cooperation with the Spirit is not limited solely to giving a body to the humanity of Jesus but continues today in building the body of Christ, which is the Church.

In the Spirit Mary Continues to Be the Mother of the Body of Christ

The Virgin Mary, even after the birth of Christ, remained *in the power of the Annunciation,* that is, in the constant arrival of the Holy Spirit who continually makes her Mother, not only of Jesus, but of the body of Christ, which is the Church.

Mary, by giving birth to Jesus, engendered, in a certain sense, all of humanity. Christ, in fact, from the first moment of his earthly existence "recapitulates" in himself all humanity and, in a special way, all the baptized. The baptized are conceived with Christ, born with him, live, die, and rise again with him and in him because Christ "summarizes" in himself all human beings who were, are, and will be. When the Holy Virgin conceives and gives birth to Jesus Christ by virtue of the Spirit, with him and in him she conceives and engenders all those who will come because Christ from the very beginning is destined to be "the head of the body, the Church" (Col. 1:18). This finality will be achieved after the resurrection and Pentecost. This is why Jesus from the moment of his birth "summarizes" in himself all of humanity. St. Basil calls the birthday of Christ, and not only metaphorically, the "birthday of humanity" (*Homily on the Birth of Christ*). The same concept is affirmed by Nicholas Cabasilas. "The birth of the head [Christ] represents also the birth of the blessed members, because the members do not exist if the head is not born" (*Life in Christ*, IV, 4).

Mary becomes even more so the Mother of the Church in the Upper Room and at the foot the cross. "And so, in the redemptive economy of grace brought about through the action of the Holy Spirit, there is a unique correspondence between the moment of the incarnation of the Word and the moment of the birth of the Church. The person who links these two moments is Mary: Mary at Nazareth and Mary in the Upper Room at Jerusalem. In both cases her discreet yet essential presence indicates the path of 'birth from the Holy Spirit.' Thus she who is present in the mystery of Christ as mother becomes — by the will of the Holy Spirit — present in the mystery of the Church. In the Church too she continues to be a maternal presence, as is shown by the words spoken from the cross: 'Woman, behold your son!'; 'Behold, your mother" (*RMa*, 24).

By being assumed into heaven to be with her Son, Mary continually engenders "spiritually," that is, in the Spirit, Christ in his members. In this sense we can say that Mary is the "Mother of the Church," because in virtue of the Spirit she continues to engender the mystical body of Christ, which is the Church and every believer. "This motherhood of Mary in the order of grace continues uninterrupted...until the eternal fulfillment of all the elect" (*LG*, 62).

The Spirit is always at the core of the maternity of Mary extended to all people. Everything in the order of grace, in fact, is merited by Christ and applied by the Spirit. But in the "horizontal" distribution of grace the Spirit radiates his sanctifying power through "spiritualized" persons, and no one more than Mary, who is the *pneumatophoros* (bearer of the Spirit) to the highest degree, can contribute to transforming persons in Christ, that is, to "Christifying" them. Mary has, therefore, a primary role in the birth of Jesus and of his ecclesial body. The latter takes place always in the power of the Spirit, which also endows her with a share in the power of the intercession of the Spirit. Thus as Mary is in the Upper Room, among the apostles, "by her prayers imploring the gift of the Spirit" (*LG*, 59), so in glory does she pray and intercede for everyone. In like manner, as the Spirit prays and intercedes in us (see Rom. 8:15–16) and is our *Advocate* and *Counsellor* (see John 14:16, 26), Mary also, as 'bride of the Spirit," continues to intercede so that the Father permanently sends the Spirit to his Church, and it is the Spirit who transforms people in Jesus the Son. Along with the Spirit, she says, "Come, Lord," hoping that even the last of her children will reach the house of the Father.

Conclusion

As John Paul II exhorts: "Mary, who conceived the incarnate Word by the power of the Holy Spirit and then in the whole of her life allowed herself to be guided by his interior activity, will be contemplated and imitated during this year above all as the woman who was docile to the voice of the Spirit, a woman of silence and attentiveness, a woman of hope who, like Abraham, accepted God's will 'hoping against hope' (see Rom. 4:18). Mary gave full expression to the longing of the poor of Yahweh and is a radiant model for those who entrust themselves with all their hearts to the promises of God" (*TMA*, 48).

The Spirit, who made Mary an incomparable masterpiece,

at the same time continually teaches and educates the Church to venerate the Virgin (see *LG*, 53). This must give rise to a Marian religious instruction and piety which does not sin through defect or excess. Mary has an indispensable place in the economy of salvation. She was the one "to render Christ our brother" (St. Francis), but without the extraordinary action of the Spirit she might have remained an anonymous woman of Palestine. Furthermore, her free and loving collaboration with the Spirit makes her a model of every relationship with the sanctifying Holy Spirit.

Mary will always remain the model and prototype of the Church as regards her *maternity*. Mary was fertile only by the power of the Spirit. If the Church wants to be fertile, in daily holiness, from an existential and sacramental viewpoint, it must continually renew itself in the Spirit. As the Spirit mysteriously fertilized the Virgin and engendered Christ, so does he continually fertilize Christ's bride, the Church. And if Mary collaborates with the Spirit so that this generation takes place, so must the Church docilely make itself available to him to become the "mother of saints and martyrs."

This is true for the Church as a whole and also for every individual Christian. For Jesus to be born in every soul and continue the mystery of the *Theotokos* (God-bearer), the Creator must put himself into the very hearts of his creatures and the divine Spirit must overshadow them. St. Gregory of Nyssa writes: "That which was corporally realized in Mary, the fullness of divinity, shines in the Virgin through Christ. In a similar manner, it is realized (through the Spirit) in all purified souls. The Lord no longer comes corporally because 'we no longer know the Lord according to the flesh,' but he lives spiritually, and the Father, as the Gospel witnesses, finds his resting place with him in us. Thus the infant Jesus is born again in each of us" (*On Virginity*, II). Elsewhere the same

author affirms: "So that the provisions of the Gospel and
the activity of the Holy Spirit develop in us, Christ must be
born in us" (*Against Eunomius*, III). To give birth to Christ
in us, as Mary did, might be the best way to celebrate the
Great Jubilee, the great remembrance of these two thousand
years since the birth of Christ by the Virgin Mary through
the work of the Holy Spirit.

Let us reread the beautiful prayer written by St. Ildephon-
sus of Toledo, who refers precisely to the birth of Christ
in the soul through the Spirit: "I pray, I pray, O Holy Virgin, that I should have Jesus by that same Spirit by which
you engendered Jesus. May my soul receive Jesus, by the
work of that Spirit through whom your flesh conceived Jesus
himself.... May I love Jesus in that same Spirit in whom you
worship him as Lord and contemplate him as Son" (*On the
Perpetual Virginity of Blessed Mary*, 12).

Chapter 7

The Holy Spirit in the Liturgy

The work of human salvation was accomplished through Jesus Christ. He was incarnated, born, lived, died, and rose again for every human being. All of this was accomplished in the power of the Holy Spirit.

Since the salvific actions of Christ were fulfilled twenty centuries ago, the "task" of the Spirit has been that of making visibly present the resurrected Christ "through signs," so that Christ's salvific actions — his birth, life, teaching, miracles, and above all his death and resurrection — become "contemporary" to people. The action capable of activating the "mysteries" (salvific actions) of Christ in the Church today is called the *sacred liturgy*. The action of the Spirit is more evident than ever in the liturgy, which "is the summary of the entire economy of salvation," as St. Theodore of Studios (d. 826) affirms (see *Antirrhetica*, I, 10). In fact, the confirmation of what we are saying is found in the liturgy. Of course, the entire Holy Trinity acts in the liturgy. The Son made flesh is the living center of the liturgy, the Father is its origin and termination, but it is the Spirit who makes Christ present and contemporary in the Church.

"In the liturgy the Holy Spirit is the teacher of the faith of the People of God and artisan of 'God's masterpiece,' the sacraments of the New Covenant. The desire and work of the Spirit in the heart of the Church is that we may live from the life of the risen Christ. When the Spirit encounters in us the response of faith which he has aroused in us, he brings about genuine cooperation. Through it, the liturgy becomes the common work of the Holy Spirit and the Church.

"In his sacramental dispensation of Christ's mystery the Holy Spirit acts in the same way as at other times in the economy of salvation: he prepares the Church to encounter her Lord; he recalls and makes Christ manifest to the faith of the assembly. By his transforming power, he makes the mystery of Christ present here and now. Finally the Spirit of communion unites the Church to the life and mission of Christ" (*CCC*, 1091–92).

It is useful to reflect in a more detailed manner on the Spirit's action in the liturgy.

The Holy Spirit, Soul of the Liturgy

The Liturgy Perpetuates Pentecost

The liturgy is called "the sacrament of the Spirit" because, as in Pentecost, he fills the liturgical actions with himself. Precisely because of this previous presence of the Spirit, the liturgy becomes the place where Christ is offered. All the mysteries of the life of Christ and especially his paschal mystery — we can also say all of history from creation to the second coming of Christ — become for the believer real and effective in the liturgy. The Spirit operating in the "era of the Church" (called also the "era of the Spirit") renders Christ alive again among us. By the living force of the Spirit, the memory of Christ's passion and Easter represents more than a pious remembrance and immersion in the past: the reality of the past and the anticipation of the future become "anamneses" and "memorials," that is, live and real representations lived in the present moment of history. The believer "today" by action of the Spirit is projected toward the point of encounter of time with eternity and becomes contemporaneous with the mystery of salvation.

With the so-called *epiclesis,* the Church invokes the presence of the Spirit in the liturgy so that the mystery of salvation is reactualized. This comes about during the liturgical action when the priest through his supplication (*epiclesis*) invokes the Father to send his Spirit to make present, in signs and words, Christ and his salvific actions (the sacraments) for the glory of God and the sanctification of human beings. "Pay attention. It is God that gives the Holy Spirit. This is not a human work. The Spirit is not given as a gift by a man, but is invoked by the priest and transmitted by God. The gift of God and the ministry of the priest consists of this," affirms St. Ambrose (*On the Holy Spirit*, I, 90). Christ, after his passage to the Father, returns and is *present in the Spirit*, through whom the presence of Christ in the liturgy is linked to the power of the *epiclesis*, always heard by God. This comes to pass in a special way in the Eucharist. But the entire liturgy and the sacraments themselves exist and operate only under the sign and efficacy of the *epiclesis* which makes of the liturgy a perennial Pentecost.

The Spirit in the Liturgy Makes Present the Past

"Christian liturgy not only recalls the events that saved us but actualizes them, makes them present. The paschal mystery of Christ is celebrated, not repeated. It is the celebrations that are repeated, and in each celebration there is an outpouring of the Holy Spirit that makes the unique mystery present" (*CCC*, 1104). This is why at Christmas we can sing in truth and without pretense: "Today, Christ is born!" As St. Leo the Great (d. 461) attests: "All that was visible in Christ has passed into the sacraments of the Church [in the liturgy]" (*Sermons*, LXXIV, 2). In liturgical language, to celebrate the past in order to make it present through the action of the Spirit is called *anamnesis*, which means "commemoration." But the Spirit in the liturgy does not limit himself to "commemorating" with the Word what Christ has done for his people. He makes it actually present to the assembly in the celebration.

The Spirit in the Liturgy Gives a Foretaste of the Future

Our Orthodox brothers and sisters define the liturgy as "heaven on earth." It is nothing less than an "icon" of the heavenly liturgy celebrated by the High and Eternal priest, Christ the Lord (see the letter to the Hebrews). The anamnesis is not only the celebration-commemoration of a past reality, but also of future events, that is the reign of God to come. "The Holy Spirit's transforming power in the liturgy hastens the coming of the kingdom and the consummation of the mystery of salvation. While we wait in hope he causes us really to anticipate the fullness of communion with the Holy Trinity" (CCC, 1107). Because of this, the liturgy is a prefiguring sign which indicates the future Kingdom of God, the terminal point of salvation.

The Spirit in the Liturgy Gathers the Faithful in Unity

The liturgy, especially the Eucharist, is the *synaxis* (the assembly of the faithful), which, scattered and disunited, gathers as the apostles did at Pentecost "all together in one place" (Acts 2:1). The "gathering together in unity," in other words, in the Church (the assembly, the people called together), is the work of the Father and is realized by becoming the body of Christ. But it is the Spirit who bonds the scattered people in unity because he is personally communicated to each individual and transforms the many into the living body of Christ. Thus, he is the creator of the People of God, the people of the new and eternal worship of the Father, a living temple and the preeminent place of glorification of the Trinity. "For it is we who are the circumcision, who worship in the Spirit of God and boast in Christ Jesus and have no confidence in the flesh," affirms St. Paul (Phil. 3:3). "In every liturgical action the Holy Spirit is sent in order to bring us into communion with Christ and so to form his body. The Holy Spirit is like the sap of the Father's vine which bears fruit on its branches. The most intimate cooperation of the Holy Spirit and the Church is achieved in the liturgy. The Spirit, who is the Spirit of communion, abides indefectibly in the Church. For this reason the Church is the great sacrament of divine communion which gathers God's scattered children together. Communion with the Holy Trinity and fraternal communion are inseparably the fruit of the Spirit in the liturgy" (CCC, 1108).

The Spirit in the Liturgy Brings the Word to Life

The Word of God, read and listened to in the liturgy, possesses a special vitality and a real effectiveness. It becomes alive in the Spirit as if in that very moment it was pronounced by the Lord who, asking for the faith of the Christian, invites believers to respond to him with their own lives. The Word could not be accepted by the faithful without the Spirit's action because he is the welcoming of the Word in their hearts. "The Holy Spirit gives a spiritual understanding of the Word of God to those who read or hear it, according to the dispositions of their hearts. By means of the words, actions, and symbols that form the structure of a celebration, the Spirit puts both the faithful and the ministers into a living relationship with Christ, the Word and Image of the Father, so that they can live out the meaning of what they hear, contemplate, and do in the celebration.... The proclamation does not stop with a teaching; it elicits the response of faith as consent and commitment, directed at the covenant between God and his people. Once again it is the Holy Spirit who gives the grace of faith, strengthens it, and makes it grow in the community" (CCC, 1101–2).

The Presence and Action of the Spirit in the Sacraments

"Our mysteries [the sacraments] are not like a theatrical performance. Here everything is controlled by the Spirit," said St. John Chrysostom (*Homily on 1 Corinthians*, 41:4). The Holy Spirit, through the Church's sacraments, puts us in a lively and efficacious contact with the Savior and his salvific work. As Christ fulfilled salvation in the Spirit, so that same salvation is applied to every believer by Christ in his Spirit, who not only makes the sacraments possible but "permits every one of us to accept the mysteries of Christ" (Nicholas Cabasilas, *Life in Christ*, II, 4, 6). "Sacraments are 'powers that come forth' from the body of Christ, which is ever-living and life-giving. They are actions of the Holy Spirit at work in his body, the Church" (CCC, 1116). Their effectiveness derives solely from the Spirit because he "always transforms that which he touches" (Cyril of Jerusalem, *Catecheses*, V, 7). St. Isidore of Seville said: "Only in the Church are the sacraments fruitfully celebrated. In fact, it is the Holy Spirit who lives in them and secretly works their effects" (*Etymologies*, VI, 19, 40–41). Within this outline, we will spend some time examining the action of the Spirit in the sacraments of Christian initiation: Baptism, Confirmation, and the Eucharist.

Baptism

The *Catechism* says: "Holy Baptism is the basis of the whole Christian life, the gateway to life in the Spirit (*vitae spiritualis ianua*), and the door which gives access to the other sacraments. Through Baptism we are freed from sin and reborn as sons of God; we become members of Christ, are incorporated into the Church and made sharers of her mission" (CCC, 1213).

The action of the Spirit in Baptism can be received, therefore, in the full power of this sacrament.

BAPTISM REGENERATES US IN THE SPIRIT. Above all, Baptism is seen as "the water of rebirth and renewal by the Spirit" (Titus 3:5). Novatian summarizes the doctrine of Baptism in this way: "The Holy Spirit performs the second birth in water. He is the seed of the divine family and the one who consecrates us to heavenly life, the pledge of our hereditary promise and like a hand-written testament of eternal salvation. He makes us into temples of God and his dwelling place. He lives in our bodies as the author of holiness. Acting in this way in us, he enables our bodies to progress toward immortal resurrection" (*On the Trinity*, 29, 16). Thus, through Baptism the Spirit performs such a radical renewal that it can be compared to a true and proper *rebirth* (see 2 Cor. 5:17). As it is true that without a biological birth human beings cannot exist, so without the birth through Baptism we cannot enter into the kingdom of heaven because Baptism is a true and proper "birth in the Spirit." Christ's words to Nicodemus clearly express this "spiritual" meaning of Baptism: "Very truly I tell you, no one can enter the kingdom of God without being born of water and Spirit. What is born of the flesh is flesh, and what is born of the Spirit is spirit" (John 3:5-6). This is why Christian tradition compares baptismal water, fertilized by the Spirit, to the mother's womb which generates life. For the Syrian theologian Theodore of Mopsuestia, to be reborn it was "necessary for the priest to ask God to send the grace of the Holy Spirit over the water to make it the womb of a spiritual birth, because Christ said to Nicodemus, if you are not born of water and the Holy Spirit you cannot enter the Kingdom of heaven (see John 3:5). In carnal birth the maternal womb receives a seed, which the divine hand then molds. In the same way, in Baptism the water becomes a womb for the person to be born, but it is by the grace of the Holy Spirit that the baptized person is baptized for a second birth" (*Catechetical Sermons*, XIV, 9). For St. Leo the Great, there is an analogy between Christian Baptism and the conception of Christ: "It is Christ, born of the Holy Spirit and a virgin mother, who fertilizes with his breath the immaculate Church because through the birth of Baptism the multitudinous children of God are born" (*Catechetical Sermons*, LXIII, 6).

IN BAPTISM WE ARE JUSTIFIED IN THE SPIRIT. The first effect of this regeneration is to be free from sin and justified: "But you were washed, you were sanctified, you were justified in the name of the Lord Jesus Christ and in the Spirit" (1 Cor. 6:11). This is not simply a freedom from sin, but a true and proper "death to sin" to "be born in a new life." Both the Eastern and Western Fathers, following the typology of the baptismal immersion in water, consider water as a symbol of death and the Spirit as an agent of life. St. Basil the Great says: "Baptism has a double aim: to abolish the body of sin so that we may not bear fruit unto death; to live in the Spirit and produce the fruits of holiness. Water offers the image of death receiving the body as if in a tomb. The Spirit instills life-giving power, renewing our life from the state of the death of sin to the state of original life. This means to be reborn from on high, from the water and the Spirit; we die in water but the Spirit gives us life" (*On the Holy Spirit*, XV, 35). St. Ambrose of Milan echoes this: "Water, in fact, is the image of death, while the Spirit is the pledge of life, in such a way that the body of sin dies in the water, which closes in on sin as if a sealed tomb. By virtue of the Spirit we are renewed from the death of sin.... Therefore, if there is grace in the water, this does not stem from the nature of the water, but from the presence of the Spirit" (*On the Holy Spirit*, I, 76–77).

Furthermore, the salvation of Christ given by the Spirit in Baptism consists in the empowering of the "theological virtues" — faith, hope, and charity, and especially charity, which includes the other two. Inspired by the Pauline text, "God's love has been poured into our hearts through the Holy Spirit that has been given to us"(Rom. 5:5), the Fathers often identified the charity of God in the faithful (the love of God for them and the possibility to respond to this love) with the presence of the Holy Spirit. The text of St. Augustine is famous: "The love which is from God and which is God is properly, therefore, of the Holy Spirit through whom the charity of God is poured into our hearts and by whom the entire Trinity lives in us" (*On the Trinity*, XV, 18, 32).

This new life which the Spirit pours into believers through Baptism is *life in Christ*.

IN THE SPIRIT WE ARE INCORPORATED INTO CHRIST AND INTO THE CHURCH. As baptized, you "have clothed yourselves with Christ," affirms St. Paul (Gal. 3:27). This is not only an exterior union, but rather an insertion into his body, into his person, to become one with him. This unity with Christ also brings about the union of all the baptized, a miracle made possible only in the Spirit who creates "the mystical body" of Christ: "For in the one Spirit we were all baptized into one body — Jews or Greeks, slaves or free — and we were all made to drink of one Spirit" (1 Cor. 12:13). Only by being in Christ through the Spirit is it possible to become "children of God in the Son" (see Gal. 4:5–7), to participate in the nature of God (see 2 Pet. 1:4), to become co-inheritors with him (see Rom. 8:17), and to form the Holy Church of God by being a temple of the Spirit (see 1 Cor. 6:19). By participating in the death of Christ, we can also share in the resurrection (see Rom. 6:3–4): "Baptism makes us members of the body of Christ: 'Therefore ... we are members of one another' (Eph. 4:25). Baptism incorporates us *into the Church*. From the baptismal fonts is born the one People of God of the New Covenant, which transcends all the natural or human limits of nations, cultures, races, and sexes" (*CCC*, 1267).

IN BAPTISM WE ARE IMPRINTED WITH A SPIRITUAL SEAL. The doctrine of a "spiritual seal" imprinted on Christians at Baptism was already a solid one among the Latin Fathers. The Spirit imprints Christ into Christians, conforming them to him. St. Ambrose, interpreting Ephesians 1:13–14, writes of Baptism: "We have been, therefore, sealed with the Spirit of God. Just as Christ died to be reborn, so are we sealed with the Spirit so that we can obtain the splendor, image, and grace which is, clearly, the seal of the Spirit. In fact, even though we were visibly sealed in our bodies, in reality we are sealed in our hearts because the Holy Spirit reproduces in us the outline of the image of the celestial man" (*On the Holy Spirit*, I, 79). The *Catechism* recalls: "Incorporated into Christ by Baptism, the person baptized is configured to Christ. Baptism seals the Christian with the indelible spiritual mark (character) of his belonging to Christ" (*CCC*, 1272).

THE BAPTISM OF THE LORD PREFIGURES THAT OF CHRISTIANS. The role of the Holy Spirit is clear at Jesus' baptism in the Jordan River. Precisely at the moment in which John baptizes Jesus, "God anointed Jesus of Nazareth with the Holy Spirit and with power" (Acts 10:38). On that occasion Jesus was manifested as the Anointed One, the Christ, the Messiah. It was then that "suddenly the heavens were open to him and he saw the Spirit of God descending like a dove and alighting on him" (Matt. 3:16). This is why the baptism of the Lord is called a theophany, the manifestation of the three persons in their unanimous witness.

In their baptism Christians are incorporated into Christ by

the Holy Spirit. They are "anointed" by the Spirit, "Christified" and sanctified. Cyril of Jerusalem affirms: "Baptized in Christ and having clothed yourselves in Christ, you have become configured to the Son of God. As we are predestined to adoption as children, God has configured us to the glorious body of Christ. As you participate in Christ you are justly called Christs... because you have received the seal of the Holy Spirit. Everything has been done to you in images because you are images of Christ. After being baptized in the Jordan and communicating his divine perfume to the water, Christ came out and the Holy Spirit personally descended upon him, like upon like. When you came out of the water of the sacred font, you were likewise confirmed with chrism, symbolizing the Holy Spirit anointing Christ" (*Catecheses*, XXI, 1).

Confirmation

In the tradition of the Church "Confirmation" is the preeminent sacrament of the Spirit. Yet this sacrament can be understood and lived only in relation to Baptism and the Eucharist. "Baptism, the Eucharist, and the sacrament of Confirmation together constitute the 'sacraments of Christian initiation,' whose unity must be safeguarded" (CCC, 1285). In the Eastern tradition, Confirmation is conferred together with Baptism. "In the West the desire to reserve the completion of Baptism to the bishop caused the temporal separation of the two sacraments" (CCC, 1290, 1300). We can say, along with St. Cyprian, that Baptism is a "double sacrament," even though Baptism and Confirmation are distinct without being separate. The two have a relationship of distinction-continuity because out of both flows the Spirit, but with a different aim.

It has been noted regarding Baptism that we are filled with the Spirit and thus transformed into Christ. But receiving the

Spirit in Baptism is not a conclusive or definitive act. The Spirit is the love of God *personified,* given to put humanity in communion with the tripersonal divine life. This self-giving of God in his Spirit is never completed because the life of God is inexhaustible and infinite. For this reason the Spirit gives himself to human beings in different sacraments, with different signs and for different purposes, even if the final objective of every intervention of the Spirit is always communion with God. What changes are the diversity of the signs and the words in the various sacraments and the immediate functions that each develops in the life of the faithful. Thus is it possible to understand the intimate union between Baptism and Confirmation, as well as their diversity.

WITH CONFIRMATION WE PARTICIPATE IN PENTECOST. The Spirit was poured forth upon Jesus during different moments of his earthly life, especially at Baptism, transforming him into the Christ (the Anointed One, Messiah and Savior). At Pentecost the Spirit turned toward the new People of God as an eschatological sign of messianic times (see Ezek. 36:25–27; Gal. 3:1–2) and fulfilled the promise of Christ (Luke 12:12; John 3:5–8). According to the teaching of Paul VI: "Since that time the apostles, in fulfilling the will of Christ, communicated the gift of the Spirit to the newly initiated through the imposition of hands, destined to complete the grace of Baptism.... This imposition of hands is rightly considered by Catholic tradition as the origin of the Sacrament of Confirmation, which in a certain sense renders the grace of Pentecost a perennial event in the Church" (*Divinae Consortium Naturae*). For the faithful Confirmation represents the mystery of Pentecost that follows the passion and Easter, mysteries especially lived in Baptism. If Pentecost signals the extraordinary and official entrance of the early Church into the world, Confirmation signals the Spirit uniting the baptized with a new bond to Christ the head, making them participate in his messianic investiture according to his triple power as priest, king, and prophet.

IN CONFIRMATION WE ARE SEALED IN THE SPIRIT. During Confirmation we are anointed with the sacred "chrism," consecrated by the bishop on Holy Thursday with the words: "Receive the seal of the gift of the Spirit." Even more clearly, the baptized person is "marked," like Christ in the Jordan, by the holy and indelible seal which is the Holy Spirit: "But it is God who establishes us with you in Christ and has anointed us by putting his seal on us and giving us his Spirit in our hearts as a first installment" (2 Cor. 1:21–22). "This seal of the Holy Spirit marks our total belonging to Christ, our enrollment in his service for ever, as well as the promise of divine protection in the great eschatological trial" (*CCC,* 1296). The Church Fathers never tired of explaining to the catechumens the rich significance of this unction (anointing). St. Athanasius writes: "The Spirit is defined as unction and seal.... The unction has the perfume and smell of him who anoints in such a way that the anointed ones participate and say 'we are the aroma of Christ' (2 Cor. 2:15). The seal has the form of Christ and all who are sealed take the same form.... Through the Spirit we are called participators in God" (*Letter to Serapion,* I, 23–24).

THROUGH CONFIRMATION THE SPIRIT HELPS CHRISTIANS GROW IN CHRIST. A typical concept of the Church Fathers is the distinction between "image" and "likeness." "Image" refers to being and "likeness" to action. "Image" indicates the ontological moment and refers to the nature of human beings insofar as they participate in divine nature through their re-creation in redemption-Baptism. "Likeness" alludes to the existential moment and recalls the life-giving logic of the image which drives nature, offered as a gift to humanity. The "likeness" evolves and fulfills itself according to God's design, acting out what is inherent in it and maturing the seeds placed in it. The active sense of "likeness" signifies an unceasing need to grow and a personal effort to mature, sustained and carried forward by grace. In Baptism the Spirit reconstructs human beings, deformed by sin, into the image of God. With Confirmation, he confers likeness. This is why Confirmation can be defined as the sacrament of "fullness" because it confers the gift of perfection and holiness. Through the first sacrament (Baptism) we enter into divine being and now we are made capable of divine action thanks to the power of the Spirit.

THE SPIRIT CONFERS HIS SEVEN GIFTS THROUGH CONFIRMATION. In Confirmation the connection with the action of the Spirit is especially evident in its ties to holiness and "chrism" (unction). It is the preeminent sacrament which confers the gifts of the Spirit, the very *fullness* of the Spirit himself. In theology, "gifts of the Spirit" has a double denotation: the first, equivalent to a "charism," is a manifestation of the Spirit in a person to build the Church (this is the reasoning of 1 Cor. 12); the second is that of the spiritual "gift," superior even to infused virtue. These "gifts" are, at the same time, manifestations of the Spirit living in the faithful and expressions of the great dynamism moving toward an ever more profound intimacy with the Spirit. The teachings of the liturgy, patristic tradition, and theology deduce the seven gifts of the Holy Spirit from the messianic text of Isaiah 11:1–2: "A shoot shall come out from the stump of Jesse, and a branch shall grow out of his roots. The spirit of the Lord shall rest on him, the spirit of wisdom and understanding, the spirit of counsel and might, the spirit of knowledge and fear of the Lord." (The "spirit of piety" will be added only by the Vulgate.)

Thus in the Pentecost Sequence, "Veni Sancte Spiritus," the Church prays: "Give to your faithful — who trust in you — your seven holy gifts." In the hymn *Veni Creator,* the

Spirit-Paraclete is invoked: "Tu septiformis munere" ("You sevenfold in your gift").

In his exhortation of Christians, St. Ambrose says: "Remember that you have received the spiritual seal, 'the Spirit of wisdom and intelligence, the Spirit of counsel and fortitude, the Spirit of understanding and piety, the Spirit of fear of God.' Preserve what you have received. God the Father has placed his seal on you. He has confirmed you in Christ the Lord. And he has placed in your heart the pledge of the Spirit" (*On the Mysteries*, 7, 42). Taking up this tradition, the *Catechism of the Catholic Church* affirms: "The seven gifts of the Holy Spirit are wisdom, understanding, counsel, fortitude, knowledge, piety, and fear of the Lord. They belong in their fullness to Christ, Son of David. They complete and perfect the virtues of those who receive them. They make the faithful docile in readily obeying divine inspirations" (*CCC*, 1831).

These "gifts" of the Spirit produce that special strength by which those confirmed, incorporated more intimately into the Church, are called to be "witnesses" to their faith and to defend it with word and deed. "By the sacrament of Confirmation they [the baptized] are more perfectly bound to the Church and are endowed with the special strength of the Holy Spirit. Hence they are, as true witnesses of Christ, more strictly obliged to spread the faith by word and deed" (*LG*, 1). This is why in the early Christian centuries, when the martyrs and those ready to die for Christ were considered to be the "true Christians," the Holy Spirit was experienced as the one who assisted the "martyrs" (witnesses in giving testimony of their faith and their love for Christ when facing the executioner).

The Eucharist

The Eucharist is more than "the source and summit of the Christian life" (*LG,* 11). It is also the synthesis of life in the faith. This is why St. Irenaeus can say: "Our doctrine is in keeping with the Eucharist, and the Eucharist confirms it" (*Against Heresies,* IV, 18, 5). Vatican II says that "in the most blessed Eucharist is contained the whole spiritual good of the Church, namely, Christ himself our Pasch" (*PO,* 5). Because the Eucharist contains this reality in itself, the action of the Holy Spirit is nowhere else in the liturgy as evident as it is here. This presence and action of the Spirit in the Eucharist is summarized in the Anaphora of Hippolytus of Rome, in which this prayer is addressed to God the Father: "Make your Holy Spirit descend on the offering of your holy Church, and after having gathered the saints, allow them all as they receive it to be filled with the Holy Spirit to fortify themselves in the faith and in truth so that we can praise and glorify you through your son Jesus Christ, through whom comes your glory and honor, Father and Son with the Holy Spirit in your Holy Church now and forever" (*Apostolic Tradition,* 4).

THE SPIRIT MAKES CHRIST PRESENT IN THE EUCHARIST. The Lord Jesus is certainly present in the Eucharist. This presence is dynamic, not static, because in it we celebrate the *anamnesis* of all the mysteries of Christ. Patriarch Germanus I of Constantinople (d. 738), after having mentioned the *anamnesis* — Jesus' incarnation, passion, resurrection, final coming — writes of the Incarnation: " 'From the womb of the morning, like dew, your youth will come to you' (Ps. 110:3). The priest implores you anew to fulfil the mystery of your Son, that he be generated transforming the bread and wine into the body and blood of Christ and God so that today is accomplished the 'I have begotten you' (Ps. 2:7). Thus, the Holy Spirit, invisibly present by the consent of the Father and the will of the Son, shows divine energy and, through the hand of the priest, consecrates and converts the holy gifts presented into the body and blood of our Lord Jesus Christ, who said 'I sanctify myself, so that they also may be sanctified in truth' (John 17:19). How? 'Just as the living Father sent me, and I live because of the Father, so whoever eats me will live because of me' (John 6:57)" (*Ecclesiastical and Mystagogical History*). A Catholic theologian, M. J. Scheeben, summarizes the voice of tradition: "The Eucharist is the real and universal continuation and amplification of the mystery of the incarnation. The eucharistic presence of Christ itself is already a reflection and amplification of his incarnation.... The changing of the bread to the body of Christ by action of the Holy Spirit is a renewing of the marvelous act with which he originally formed his body in the womb of the Virgin by virtue of the same Holy Spirit and absorbed it into his person. Just as by this act he entered for the first time into the world, so in that change he multiplies his substantial presence through space and time" (*Mysteries of Christianity*).

THE SPIRIT IN THE EUCHARIST ACTUALIZES THE PASCHAL MYSTERY. "At the Last Supper, on the night he was betrayed, our Savior instituted the eucharistic sacrifice of his Body and Blood. This he did in order to perpetuate the sacrifice of the cross throughout the ages until he should come again, and so to entrust his beloved Spouse, the Church, a memorial of his death and resurrection: a sacrament of love, a sign of unity, a bond of charity, a paschal banquet" (*SC*, 47).

According to Vatican II's teaching, the mystery of the death and resurrection of Christ constitutes the culmination of the entire history of salvation and the entire history of humanity. From this mystery Christian hope arises because the new life of Christ's resurrection is given in the Eucharist through the action of the Spirit. "For in the most blessed Eucharist is contained the whole spiritual good of the Church, namely, Christ himself our Pasch and the living bread which gives life through his flesh — that flesh which is given life and gives life through the Holy Spirit" (*PO, 5*). The Spirit has transformed the death of Christ into an offering of filial love for the Father and for the salvation of humanity and has raised him from the dead. In the same way, the Spirit in the Eucharist reactualizes this mystery of love so that its fruits can be enjoyed. Through the work of the Spirit it is possible to participate in the redeeming death of Christ and his resurrection. In analogical fashion, Theodore of Mopsuestia develops this parallelism between the intervention of the Spirit in the resurrection of Christ and his intervention in the Eucharist. "According to the liturgical formulas, the priest must supplicate God to send the Holy Spirit over the bread and wine so that in this commemoration of immortality the body and blood of our Lord might truly appear. The natural body of our Lord was as mortal as ours. But through the resurrection it became immortal and unchangeable. And when our High Priest declares that this bread and wine is the body and blood of Christ, he reveals that they have become so through contact with the Holy Spirit. This occurs now as in the natural body of Christ when you receive the Holy Spirit and his anointing. In the same way, even now, when the Holy Spirit comes, we regard it that the bread and wine offered receive a special anointing through the grace placed upon them" (*Catechetical Sermons*, XVI, 12).

PENTECOST IS CONTINUED IN THE EUCHARIST. The Spirit's presence in the Eucharist makes the celebration of this sacrament a Pentecost, an efficacious descent of the Spirit. The Pentecostal character of the Eucharist is more than evident in the various rites, especially the Eastern ones, and also in the Fathers and the ecclesial writers. The eucharistic *epiclesis* (invocation to the Father to send his Spirit to transform the bread and wine into the body and blood of Christ) summarizes the entire history of salvation, from creation to the Parousia. It unites the three movements of the work of salvation: the cross, the resurrection, and Pentecost. Innumerable texts speak of the eucharistic *epiclesis* as a Pentecostal descent of the Spirit, an indispensable condition for the eucharistic presence of Christ.

We see this in the new Eucharistic Prayers of the Roman Missal, for example: "We ask you to make [these gifts] holy by the power of your Spirit, so that they may become the body and blood of your Son, our Lord Jesus Christ, at whose command we celebrate this Eucharist."

The ancient tradition of the Church especially insists on the necessity of this presence of the Spirit so that the miracle of the transformation of the bread and wine into the body and blood of Christ takes place. The same principle inspires the Fathers: the Holy Spirit sanctifies, consecrates, transforms, and makes Christ present. Cyril of Jerusalem says: "Then, we too, sanctified through these spiritual hymns [the chant of the *Trisagion,* that is, the *Sanctus*], ask the all-giving God to send the Holy Spirit over the gifts placed here to make the bread the body of Christ and the wine the blood of Christ. Everything that the Holy Spirit touches becomes sanctified and transformed" (*Catecheses,* V, 7). There is also a text of Nicholas Cabasilas which summarizes the *epiclesis* doctrine. "Christ ordered the apostles, and through them the Church, to do thusly: 'Do this in memory of me,' he said. He could not have given such an order if he had not, at the same time, put at our disposition the only power capable of executing it. What is this power? It is the Holy Spirit, the strength which from on high fortified the apostles, according to the word of the Lord: 'Stay here in the city until you have been clothed with power from on high'

(Luke 24:49; see Acts 1:8). Here is the action of this divine presence: once descended, the Holy Spirit does not abandon us but remains with us to the end. The Savior sent him precisely so he would dwell in us forever.... It is this very same Spirit who, by the hand and tongue of the priest, consecrates the offerings. But the Lord did more than send the Holy Spirit to dwell in us; he himself promised to live with us 'to the end of the age' (Matt. 28:20). The Paraclete is invisibly present, lacking human form. But the Savior chose, by means of the divine and holy eucharistic offerings, to be seen and touched, having assumed our nature forever. Christ and the Spirit are, therefore, the priest and he who is the power of the priesthood" (*Commentary on the Divine Liturgy,* 28).

THE SPIRIT IN THE EUCHARIST GIVES A FORETASTE TASTE OF THE FUTURE KINGDOM. From the beginning, the Eucharist was seen as the "medicine of immortality," as the power which frees human beings from their worst enemy — death. The idea of the Eucharist as a source of immortality is already found in John's Gospel (see John 6:50–51, 54), then in Ignatius of Antioch, for whom the Eucharist is "the medicine of immortality, antidote preventing death and providing everlasting life in Jesus Christ" (*Letter to the Ephesians,* XX, 2). This "nourishing of immortality" in mortal bodies derives from the risen Christ when he is received in the Eucharist. But it also comes from the Spirit in whom we "satisfy our hunger" by eating the body of Christ.

In the Eucharist not only does the Spirit make present the mysteries already lived by Christ, but the risen Christ himself represents for us the *final reality,* the *eschaton,* by the very fact that the transformation of the offerings presupposes the descent of the Spirit, who with his coming brings the "last days" into history (Acts 2:17). In this way, the "eighth" day is already present in the Eucharist, eternity breaks into the present, giving us a foretaste of that which will be in eternity. During the Divine Liturgy (the eucharistic celebration) we pray standing up, affirms St. Basil. He explains this liturgical practice: "It is not only because, as risen with Christ and searching for the things from above, we remember, standing in prayer on the day dedicated to the resurrection (Sunday), the grace which has been given us. It is also because that day seems to be in some way the image of the future eternity,... the eighth day..., the eternal day without night and without tomorrow, the world without end which does not age" (*On the Holy Spirit,* XXVII, 66).

IN THE EUCHARIST, ALONG WITH CHRIST, WE RECEIVE THE HOLY SPIRIT. If in the Eucharist it is possible to unite with the Lord and become his body and his blood, it is because his "flesh" is already "spiritualized." As the Gospel of John says: "It is the spirit that gives life; the flesh is useless" (John 6:63). Thanks to the Spirit, Jesus has entered into the glory of the Father and therefore can offer himself in the Eucharist. Christians cannot receive the Eucharist if first they are not transformed by the Spirit and made worthy of this communion. Individual human beings (the "flesh") with their natural power cannot receive Christ. From this stems the necessity that in the Eucharist we also receive the Spirit so that this vital communion with the Lord can take place. The Spirit brings Christ to human beings, and Christ, in turn, brings the Spirit according to the general law of the economy of salvation. Where there is the Spirit, there is Christ, and where there is Christ, there is the Spirit. For St. Francis of Assisi it is the Holy Spirit who in believers directly receives the body of Christ: "It is the Spirit of the Lord, who dwells in his faithful, who receives the holiest body and blood of the Lord" (*Admonitions,* I).

The presence of the Spirit in the Eucharist and communion with him — indispensable condition to "communicate" with the body and blood of Christ — is evident in the Eastern liturgical traditions and hymns. This is especially true of the rich liturgical hymns of St. Ephrem of Syria (d. ca. 373). Jesus "called bread his living body, filled it with himself and the Spirit, extended his hand, and gave them the bread:... Take and eat with faith and do not doubt that this is my body. He who eats with faith, by this eats the fire of the Spirit.... Everyone eat, and through this means eat the Spirit.... From now on you will eat an Easter pure and without stain, a bread fermented and perfected, kneaded and cooked by the Spirit, a wine mixed with flame and the Spirit" (*Discourse on Holy Week*, IV, 4).

THE HOLY SPIRIT INCORPORATES US INTO THE "TOTAL CHRIST." We have seen how the Baptism of the Spirit "incorporates" the faithful to Christ and makes them Church. In the Eucharist such an incorporation grows, is nourished, and continually matures, becoming internalized and personal. Therefore, the faithful are not only united to Christ the head, but also to his members. This is a rich and profound reality for Christian life. It is impossible to communicate with Christ the head in life except in contact with his body, which is the Church. We communicate with Christ the head in the measure in which we also communicate with our brothers and sisters, just as we cannot communicate with our brothers and sisters if we are not in communion with Christ the head. The Eucharist is the sacrament creating this two-dimensional communion which, in the end, is reduced to one reality, the body of Christ, the Church. This is why we dare to say the Eucharist "builds the Church." The Spirit is always the principle of unity and cohesion in this "communion." We emphasize this in the new official Eucharistic Prayers, in which the priest, after having pronounced the words of the institution of the Eucharist, recites a second *epiclesis*. He prays to the Father to send his Spirit and make everybody into "one body, one spirit in Christ." After the resurrection and Pentecost, Christ exists only as the *total Christ*. St. Augustine writes: "If you want to understand the body of Christ, listen to the apostle who tells the faithful: 'Now you are the body of Christ and individually members of it' (1 Cor. 12:27). If you are therefore the body of Christ and his members, your sacred mystery is placed on the table of the Lord. You receive your sacred mystery. To that which you are, answer Amen, and in answering you ratify it. In fact, when you hear 'the body of Christ' answer 'Amen.' You are really the body of Christ; therefore your 'Amen' should be true! Why in the bread? Here we do not offer our ideas. Let us listen to the same apostle who, speaking of this sacrament, said: 'Because there is one bread, we who are many are one body' (1 Cor. 10:17). Understand and enjoy unity, truth, piety, and charity. 'One bread': Who is this bread? 'We who are many...one body.' Reflect. Bread is not made with just one kernel, but with many. You came stained when you received the baptismal exorcism. When you were baptized, you came as withered ones. When you received the flame of the Holy Spirit, you came away cooked. Be what you see and receive that which you are! This is what the apostle said about bread" (*Sermons*, 227, 1).

The Eucharist as communion in the Holy Spirit becomes, therefore, the "communion in the holy" in a double sense: communion in things holy and communion of holy people, that is, people sanctified by the Spirit. In this way we understand why the Eucharist is the *sacrament of love*.

In the Spirit All of Life Becomes Liturgy and Worship

St. Paul writes: "For it is we who are the circumcision, who worship in the Spirit of God and boast in Christ Jesus" (Phil. 3:3). Render "worship to God" or "adore him" in "Spirit and truth" (see John 4:24) means to be oriented with our entire being toward God, making it adhere to Christ. This vital worship is realized liturgically in the power of the Spirit, who makes of the believer a "living liturgy" in the living temple of God, which is the community brought together by the Father in Jesus Christ. In Christ, in fact, "the whole structure is joined together and grows into a holy temple in the Lord; in whom you also are built together spiritually into a dwelling place for God" (Eph. 2:21–22). Or as St. Paul says elsewhere, the Christian by means of the Spirit becomes "God's temple" (see 1 Cor. 3:16–17). The concept of temple is closely connected to that of worship, even if in the new Christian worship it is not circumscribed in any place, but is rather in the life of the Christians themselves, made living temples of the Spirit so that their entire existence is transformed into worship, praise, and glorification of God. "With gratitude in your hearts sing psalms, hymns, and spiritual songs to God. And whatever you do, in word or deed, do everything in the name of the Lord Jesus, giving thanks to God the Father through him" (Col. 3:16–17). Vatican II adopts this doctrine: "The baptized, by regeneration and the anointing of the Holy Spirit, are consecrated to be the spiritual house and a holy priesthood, that through all the works of Christian men they may offer spiritual sacrifices and proclaim the perfection of him who has called them out of the darkness into his marvelous light (see 1 Pet. 2:4–10). Therefore all the disciples of Christ, preserving in prayer and praising God (see Acts 2:42–47), should present themselves as a sacrifice, living, holy, and pleasing to God (see Rom. 12:1). They should everywhere on earth bear witness to Christ and give an answer to everyone who asks a reason for the hope of an eternal life which is theirs (see 1 Pet. 3:15)" (*LG*, 10).

Conclusion

Drawing attention to the mystery of the Holy Spirit means understanding once again the fundamental relationship that runs between the Spirit and the Church. It is the Spirit who intervenes to constitute and characterize the Church as "sacrament." The liturgical-sacramental dimension of Christian life is within the sacramental essence of the Church. Liturgical celebration, in fact, is not just communication-fulfillment of the economy of salvation but also the expression of the Christian life yet to be fulfilled. The liturgy is the summit and the source of the being of believers and, consequently, the announcement and catechesis which allows the objectives of Christian life to become one's own. It is also the sacramental gift to achieve these objectives. The liturgical-sacramental itinerary educates us about the events of Christ, whose paschal mystery is a model of the plan of Christian living. In putting the Christian mystery — "believed, professed, and lived" — at the center of celebration, the ecclesial community is able to transfigure history into the history of salvation. Also, in the liturgical-sacramental celebration the life of every believer becomes a sign of reality transformed by the grace of God. In this context, the Church's celebration of the experiences of believers by remembering the saints takes on the character of witness. The saints are those who have been able to follow in the footsteps of Christ, thus becoming the indelible sign that God acts through human beings. This year dedicated to the Holy Spirit can be providential for recovering the meaning and value of the liturgy and the sacraments of Christian initiation. John Paul II says this is especially true of Confirmation: "The primary tasks of the preparation for the Jubilee thus include a renewed appreciation for the presence and activity of the Spirit, who acts within the Church both in the sacraments, especially in Confirmation, and in a variety of charisms, roles, and ministries which he inspires for the good of the Church" (*TMA*, 45).

The sacrament of Confirmation expresses the dynamic of Christian being. By participating in the very functions of Christ and in ecclesial communion, believers authentically live their witness and, like yeast in everyday reality, are committed to building the civilization of love as a response to the crisis of civilization. "With the sacrament of Confirmation, those who are reborn in Baptism receive an ineffable gift, the Holy Spirit himself, through which they are enriched with a special power....They are more perfectly linked to the Church, while they are more strictly obliged to spread and defend, through word and deed, their faith, as authentic witnesses of Christ. Finally, Confirmation is so tied to the sacred Eucharist that the faithful, already marked by sacred Baptism and Confirmation, are inserted fully in the body of Christ through participation in the Eucharist" (Paul VI, *Divinae Consortium Naturae*).

A full recovery of the pneumatological aspect of the Eucharist could contribute to overcoming more easily the risk of limiting ourselves solely to the dimension of the *presence* of Christ, rather than to live Communion in all its richness as salvific *action* which contemplates all the mysteries of Christ. Also risky is an individualistic mentality which, in practice, reduces the Eucharist to *communion* only with Christ the head ignoring his *body*, which is the Church (see 1 Cor. 11:17–33). A "Communion" which is not a "communion" with the *total Christ* would be a flagrant contradiction of the very nature of the Eucharist, because the body of Christ is the Church and, at the same time, the sacramental body generates the mystical body.

Chapter 8

The Spirit in the Life
of Christians

It is not easy to say what the Holy Spirit is, but his action in the life of those who let themselves be transformed by him can be seen. In fact, the Spirit so transforms and transfigures the life of Christians that the profound change in their being worked by the Spirit cannot go unnoticed. The desert Fathers, when they wanted to emphasize that a monk or any baptized person was of God, simply said he or she was a *pneumatophoros,* that is, a bearer of the Spirit. Those who live under the law of the covenant are characterized by *pneumatophoria,* the bearing of the Spirit. They are deemed persons who pass from the old way of being to the new, redeemed by Jesus Christ. Unredeemed persons, on the contrary, are those who are unconnected to the Spirit, for whom darkness falls over their existence. Such persons become distanced from God. Being "strangers to the covenants of promise" they remain "alienated from the life of God" (Eph. 2:12; 4:18). "Without the Spirit we are strangers and far from God. Instead, if we participate in the Spirit we are united with Divinity," said St. Athanasius (*Orations against the Arians,* III, 24).

After treating of the mysterious action of the Spirit in the life of human beings in general and of Christians in particular, we will seek to explain the significance of his transfiguring action in the life of Christians who allow themselves "to be worked" by him who continues to sculpt the image of Christ in every baptized person.

The Spirit Makes Us Participators in the Divine Life

"The grace of the Holy Spirit has the power to justify us, that is, to cleanse us from our sins and to communicate to us 'the righteousness of God through faith in Jesus Christ' (Rom. 3:22) and through Baptism.... Through the power of the Holy Spirit we take part in Christ's passion by dying to sin, and in his resurrection by being born to a new life; we are members of his body which is the Church, branches grafted onto the vine which is himself" (*CCC*, 1987–88).

Church tradition calls this sanctifying work of the Spirit "divinization" or "deification." The expression is used especially in the Eastern Christian tradition to expressly refer to the action of the Holy Spirit. John Paul II affirms: "In divinization.... Eastern theology attributes a very special role to the Holy Spirit: through the power of the Spirit who dwells in man deification already begins on earth; the creature is transfigured and God's kingdom inaugurated" (*OL*, 6). The pope's words echo those of Athanasius: "Through the Spirit we are all called participators of God.... We enter to form part of divine nature through participation in the Spirit.... This is why the Spirit makes divine all those in which he is present" (*Letter to Serapion*, I, 14).

The Spirit's presence in human beings can also be called "sanctifying grace." If it is true that Christians are "participants of the divine nature" (2 Pet. 1:4), this is because they are "sanctified by the Spirit" (1 Pet. 1:2), as the letter to the Ephesians affirms: "Through him [Christ] both of us have access in one Spirit to the Father" (Eph 2:18). Being holy means to participate in the nature of God through Christ in the Spirit. The Father and the Son are also involved in this sanctification of human beings (see 1 Cor. 12:4–6). Human beings do not possess holiness in their substance as does God. So it is by participation in the Holy Spirit that human beings can become holy. Without the Spirit we remain "strangers and aliens." In the Spirit we become "citizens with the saints and also members of the household of God" (Eph. 2:19).

This reality obeys the dynamic of life which is constantly growing because the Holy Spirit places himself in human beings as a seed of life (see 1 John 3:9; Irenaeus, *Against Heresies*, IV, 31, 2), which slowly, with the cooperation of the person, develops until it transforms the Christian into "another Christ." St. Thomas, explaining the divine filiation of Christians, affirms: "The spiritual seed which proceeds from the Father is the Holy Spirit" (*In Rom.* c. 8, lect. 3) and citing 1 John 3:9, says: "The spiritual seed is the grace of the Holy Spirit" (*In Gal.*, c. 3, lect. 3). The Spirit, implanted in the faithful as the "seed of life," gives birth to "life in Christ" risen. It is a process of Christification in the Spirit which has a beginning, an end, and the means to guide it to maturation, to protect it, and if need be, to restore it.

The Spirit Prepares Us to Welcome the Divine Life with Faith

God the Father acts through the Spirit so that Christ lives in the heart of each person, precisely where each individual's fundamental option is born: "In him [Christ] you also, when you have heard the word of truth, the gospel of your salvation, and had believed in him, were marked with the seal of the promised Holy Spirit" (Eph. 1:13). Faith, the loving gift of God, is none other than that sublime reality from which and for which the Spirit is given and, *consequently*, life in Christ.

A constant idea in the New Testament, especially of St. Paul, says that you cannot adhere to the preaching of the Gospel without the gift of faith that is given "by the power of the Spirit of God" (see Rom. 15:19; Gal. 3:1–5; 1 Cor. 6:11; 1 Thess. 1:4–5). It follows from this that "believing is possible only by grace and the interior helps of the Holy Spirit" (CCC, 154) because this is a living faith which involves the totality of each human person and transforms the life of that person into a "life in faith." *Dei Verbum* says: "Before this faith can be exercised, man must have the interior helps of the Holy Spirit, who moves the heart and converts it to God, who opens the eyes of the mind and 'makes it easy for all to accept and believe the truth.' The same Holy Spirit constantly perfects faith by his gifts, so that revelation may be more and more profoundly understood" (*DV,* 5). The Spirit, therefore, increasingly nourishes, deepens, internalizes, and personalizes this faith. He activates the word in preaching and makes it come alive (see 1 Thess. 1:5; 4:8; 1 Pet. 1:12), helping the listener of the word and unveiling the meaning of Scripture (see 2 Cor. 3:14–15). In this way, the Spirit gives witness to Jesus so that he might be accepted in faith (see John 15:26; Acts 1:8; Rev. 19:10).

The first effect of the Spirit's animation of the faith is to make us adhere to the person of Christ with all our being, accepting him as Lord and Master in our life. The *Catechism* says: "One cannot believe in Jesus Christ without sharing in his Spirit. It is the Holy Spirit who reveals to men who Jesus is. For 'no one can say "Jesus is Lord," except by the Holy Spirit' (1 Cor. 12:3), who 'searches everything, even the depths of God. . . . No one comprehends the thoughts of God, except the Spirit of God' (1 Cor. 2:10–11). Only God knows completely; we believe in the Spirit because he is God" (CCC, 152). Faith, presupposing the cooperation of human freedom, is a gift of God, and like every gift, it is bestowed by the Spirit. St. Augustine is explicit: "The fact that we believe and act belongs to the free choice of our will. And yet both are given by the Spirit in faith and charity"

(*Retractationes,* I, 23, 2). It is clear then that "Before this faith can be exercised, man must have the interior helps of the Holy Spirit, who moves the heart and converts it to God, who opens the eyes of the mind and 'makes it easy for all to accept and believe the truth'" (*DV,* 5).

Thus Christians, animated by faith, change their attitude toward the world and reality, viewing and interpreting everything through the eyes of the Spirit. He helps us judge what things in history are opposed to the plan of salvation, and he opens our hearts to the mysteries of God so that we see life, events, and history in his light. Above all, we can understand the mystery of the cross, which otherwise would be folly for human logic. "Now we have received not the spirit of the world, but the Spirit that is from God, so that we may understand the gifts bestowed upon us by God. And we speak of these things in words not taught by human wisdom but taught by the Spirit, interpreting spiritual things to those who are spiritual" (1 Cor. 2:12–14). Christians perceive, by action of the Spirit, that the logic of faith is not based on "human wisdom," but rests on "a demonstration of the Spirit and of power" (1 Cor. 2:2–5). In other words, it is necessary to accept the heart of the Gospel, that is, the logic proper to God and opposed to that of humanity. According to God's logic, life is born from death, you rule by serving, you become free and happy to the degree that you are able to give of yourself to others without calculating or measuring the benefits for yourself. This is the path followed by Christ in his actions.

Cyril of Jerusalem described the new way with which believers see everything in the Spirit and are enabled to interpret human history: "It is like someone who was first in the darkness. After having suddenly seen the sun he has the eye of his body illuminated and sees clearly what he could not see before. Thus, those who have become worthy to receive the Holy Spirit have their souls illuminated and see in a suprahuman way that which was not seen before. The body is on earth and the soul contemplates the heavens as if in a mirror.... Each human, so small, extends his glance over the universe, from the beginning to the end, over the time in between and over the successive kingdoms. He comes to know that which no one has taught him because he is side by side with the person who illuminates him" (*Catecheses*, XV, 16).

In the Spirit We Become Children of God in the Son

The seed of life implanted in the Christian by the Spirit — welcomed and allowed to grow through faith and the sacraments — is filial life. In virtue of this the Christian, incorporated by the Spirit into Christ, the Son of God by nature, becomes a child of the Father by grace. Christians "through the Spirit reach the Son and through the Son, the Father" (St. Irenaeus, *Against Heresies*, V, 36, 2). Christians become "children in the Son," say the Fathers. St. Cyril of Jerusalem never tired of repeating the following to people preparing for Baptism: "We are worthy of invoking him as Father because of his ineffable mercy. We have been transferred from slavery to that of divine adoption not by our being children according to the nature of the heavenly Father but by the grace of the Father through the Son and the Holy Spirit" (*Catecheses*, VII, 7). St. Cyril explains this participation of humanity in divine filiation in a more elaborate theological way, spotlighting the specific roles of Christ and the Spirit: "Christ is the only Son and the firstborn Son. He is the only Son like God. By becoming human, he is the firstborn son by the salvific union he established between himself and us. Consequently, we are, in him and through him, children of God by nature and grace. By nature we are children in him and only in him. By participation and grace we are, through him, in the Spirit" (*Disquisition on the Orthodox Faith,* XXX, 27).

The ecclesiastical writers warn that we should not be misled by the expression "adoptive children." This is not a juridical affiliation but a deeper reality of physical generation. "This, precisely, is the great benefit of glorious filial adoption. This is not pure verbal sound, as in human adoption, and is not limited to conferring the honor of a name. Among us, adoptive parents transmit to their children only the name, and only by the name is the father officially their father. There is no birth nor labor pains. On the contrary, in Christianity we are dealing with a true birth and a true communion with the Only Son, not only in name but in reality: a communion of blood, flesh, and life. When the Father himself recognizes in us the members of the Only Son and discovers on our faces the effigy of his Son, what more can we be? ... Why do I speak of filial adoption? Divine adoption establishes a closer and more co-natural link than that of physical filiation, to the point that Christians reborn in the mysteries are children of God more than they are children of their own parents. Between the two births there runs a distance even greater than that between physical birth and filial adoption" (Nicholas Cabasilas, *Life in Christ,* VI).

"Life in Christ," in the Spirit, Is Expressed in a Filial Life

The Spirit not only renders us "children of the Son," but supports this *experience* by giving us *filial sentiments* which are expressed above all in prayer. "All those guided by the Spirit of God are children of God. You have not received a spirit of slavery to fall back into fear; rather you have received a spirit of adoptive children by which we can proclaim: 'Abba! Father!' The Spirit himself certifies to our spirit that we are children of God" (Rom. 8:14–16; see Gal. 4:4–7). For St. Paul the Spirit does more than make people children of God, blessing them with the gift of adoption. The Spirit also offers the experience of being such, leading us to invoke him sweetly as Father and witnessing to the divine adoption. "The Holy Spirit makes us spiritual. There is the readmission to Paradise, the return to the status of children, the courage to call God, Father. We become participators in the grace of Christ, are called children of the light, and share eternal glory" (St. Basil, *On the Holy Spirit,* XV, 36).

Christians are truly redeemed when they allow the Spirit to infuse them with spiritual filiation, a spirit of freedom and unconditional confidence. The Spirit works when we feel like infants having absolute need of a father to turn our filial prayer to, yet we do not even know enough to say the word "father." Then comes the Spirit, like a caring mother, to help us cry out with immense tenderness, "Abba! Father!" If in Romans 8:15 it is said that the children of God "cry Abba" in Galatians 4:6 it is said that "because you are children, God has sent the Spirit of his Son into our hearts crying 'Abba! Father!'" (Gal. 4:6).

The disposition of the filial soul is not a superficial thing which touches only the emotions, but springs from what is intimate in the person and originates in the discovery of the paternity of the Father revealed in Christ. It is a real and authentic divine paternity, not a metaphorical one. The Spirit makes us vividly aware of our status as children of God, a discovery which involves the most intimate energies of the spirit, making us grow and transforming us completely. In the experience of divine filiation, the Spirit reveals each human being as a "new creation" (Gal. 6:15; 2 Cor. 5:17), making each of us accept with surprise the radically new meaning of our existence as believers.

This filial disposition is existentially expressed in filial prayer and, above all, in filial obedience. Following Jesus, whose existence coincided with being son and in identifying with the will of the Father — "my food is to do the will of him who sent me and to contemplate his work" (John 4:34; see John 6:38) — the filial life of Christians guided by the Spirit will be a constant search for the will of the Father to conform to it, from love, not from fear. The Holy Spirit frees us from the fear of slavery and introduces us into the glorious freedom of the children of God (see Rom. 8:14–16; Gal. 4:4–7). Thus, in this continual conforming to the Son, the image of the Son grows and, in a parallel manner, so do filial sentiments. "Now the Lord is the Spirit, and where the Spirit of the Lord is, there is freedom. And all of us with unveiled faces, seeing the glory of the Lord as though reflected in a mirror, are being transformed into the same image from one degree of glory to another; for this comes from the Lord, the Spirit" (2 Cor. 3:17–18).

The Spirit, Master of Prayer

"The Holy Spirit, whose anointing permeates our whole being, is the interior Master of Christian prayer. He is the artisan of the living tradition of prayer. To be sure, there are as many paths of prayer as there are persons who pray, but it is the same Spirit acting in all and with all. It is in the communion of the Holy Spirit that Christian prayer is a prayer in the Church" (CCC, 2672).

The true meaning of prayer is union of the soul with God. "The life of prayer is the habit of being in the presence of the thrice-holy God and in communion with him" (CCC, 2565). St. John of Damascus said that prayer "is the elevation of the soul to God" (*On the Orthodox Faith*, III, 24). In this sense human beings on their own can only pronounce words, but they cannot "pray." Prayer as a searching for and union with God is always a gift of God himself. "We firmly believe that human nature is not able in any way to seek God and discover him with purity unless aided by the one who is being

sought. God is discovered by those who recognize him, after having done everything they could, to have need of him,"
says Origen (*Against Celsus,* VII, 42). As in any gift of God,
prayer can come only from openness to the Spirit, who puts
us in communion with the Father through the Son. "Christian prayer is a covenant relationship between God and man
in Christ. It is the action of God and of man, springing forth
from both the Holy Spirit and ourselves, wholly directed to
the Father, in union with the human will of the Son of God
made man" (CCC, 2564).

Human beings still live a fragile existence, immersed in the
uncertainty and fluctuations of time. They experience diffi-
culty in praying, unaware even what to say! But this is no
reason for discouragement because the Spirit comes to them
to take in hand the situation. The Spirit, who made us participators in the status of adopted children and to experience
this reality, is the same Spirit who now prays in us and for us.
The Spirit takes on our weakness, bringing to fulfillment the
work of salvation begun by him, despite the difficulties along
the road. "Likewise the Spirit helps us in our weakness; for
we do not know how to pray as we ought, but that very
Spirit intercedes with sighs too deep for words" (Rom. 8:26).

Christian prayer can be nothing less than filial prayer. This
is why the gift of filial adoption enacted by the Spirit is
presented by St. Paul as an experiential cry of *Abba* (that
is, "Father") (Rom. 8:15). In prayer, believers are continually becoming more aware of their own identity, called to
live a filial relationship with God the Father. "In the New
Covenant, prayer is the living relationship of the children of
God with their Father who is good beyond measure, with
his Son Jesus Christ and with the Holy Spirit. The grace
of the Kingdom is 'the union of the entire holy and royal
Trinity...with the whole human spirit.' Thus, the life of
prayer is the habit of being in the presence of the thrice-

holy God and in communion with him. This communion of life is always possible because through Baptism, we have already united with Christ. Prayer is *Christian* insofar as it is communion with Christ and extends throughout the Church, which is his Body. Its dimensions are those of Christ's love" (CCC, 2565).

Every prayer of the Christian, whether liturgical or personal, always occurs in the Spirit because access to the Father is through the Son in the Spirit (see Eph. 2:18). This helps us understand the importance of the recommendation of the letter of Jude: "But you, beloved, build yourselves up in your most holy faith; pray in the Holy Spirit; keep yourselves in the love of God" (Jude 20–21). In this sense, every form of prayer — praise, thanksgiving, supplication — is always done in the Spirit. "Be filled with the Spirit, as you sing psalms and hymns and spiritual songs among yourselves, singing and making melody to the Lord in your hearts, giving thanks to God the Father at all times and for everything in the name of our Lord Jesus Christ" (Eph. 5:18–20). Referring specifically to the prayer of intercession, St. Paul insists: "Pray in the Spirit at all times in every prayer and supplication. To that end keep alert and always preserve in supplication for all the saints" (Eph. 6:18). Only in this way does the Christian become a worshiper "in spirit and truth," as Jesus told the Samaritan woman (John 4:24). The Christian does not pray as the pagans do because Christian prayer is free and liberating, addressed to the true God, not one tied to places or objects, but one who wants to make his temple in the heart of human beings and the cosmos. Commenting on this text, St. Hilary writes: "Because God is invisible, incomprehensible, and immense, the Lord said that the time has come in which God will no longer be worshiped on a mountain or in a temple, 'for God is Spirit.' The Spirit cannot be circumscribed nor enclosed because by the power of his nature he is everywhere, absent from no place, and his fullness is superabundant in everything. Those who worship in the Spirit and truth are the true worshipers. Those who worship God — who is Spirit — in the Spirit will have God as an end and the Spirit as a means for their reverence, because each person has a different relationship toward the one to be worshiped. Saying 'God is Spirit' does not do away with the name and gift of the Holy Spirit.... The nature of the gift and honor is indicated when it is taught that it is necessary to worship God who is Spirit, in the Spirit. This reveals the type of freedom and consciousness reserved for those who worship. It also reveals the immense goal of worship because God, who is Spirit, is worshiped in the Spirit" (*On the Trinity*, II, 31).

The highest degree of prayer 'in Spirit and truth" is the one taught by the Lord Jesus himself, the Our Father, which is an authentic "spiritual" prayer. St. Cyprian writes: "He who gave us the gift of life, with the same benevolence with which he bestowed his other gifts on us, also taught us how to pray. Turning to God with the prayer dictated by the Son, we can be more easily heard. Christ already foretold that a time was to come in which the true worshipers would worship the Father 'in Spirit and truth.' He made this come to pass earlier than he promised so that we, who by virtue of his sanctification have received the Spirit and the Truth, by virtue of his action can also worship in Spirit and truth. What could be more 'spiritual' than the prayer given by Christ, he who also sent the Holy Spirit?" (*On the Lord's Prayer*, 2).

St. John Chrysostom, referring to the Our Father, affirms that he who has not received the fullness of the Spirit cannot call God by the name of Father and therefore cannot pray with the words taught by the Lord (see *Homily on the Gospel of Matthew*, XIX, 4). St. Augustine teaches: "Without him [the Spirit] whoever cries out Abba cries into the void" (*Sermons,* 71, 18).

Witnesses in the Spirit

"The Spirit's mission is also to transform the disciples into witnesses to Christ" (*CT,* 72). Jesus had affirmed: "When the Advocate comes, whom I will send to you from the Father, he will testify on my behalf. You also are to testify because you have been with me from the beginning" (John 15:26–27). To give witness to Christ in the power of the Spirit means to become involved with the Word of the Gospel so that it transforms and ferments our very existence and radiates with consistency before everyone and at whatever cost.

In the various states of Christian life in which the witness is most brilliant, the action of the Spirit is always found at the core. We see this in "witnesses" to the highest degree, that is, the "martyrs" (which in Greek means precisely, "witnesses") of yesterday and today. By being consistent in their faith and faithful to justice, the martyrs have "lost" their lives by offering them in the ultimate love of God and humanity. The early Church and the Fathers held that martyrdom was the pinnacle of holiness and was always considered the supreme gift that the Spirit gives to believers. "Why do we say that it is the Holy Spirit who infuses in martyrs the strength to witness? Do you really want to know? Because the Savior told this to his disciples: 'When they bring you before the synagogues, the rulers and the authorities, do not worry about how you are to defend yourselves or what you are to say; for the Holy Spirit will teach you at that very hour what you ought to say' (Luke 12:11–12). It is not possible to witness for Christ without the strength of the Holy Spirit. We receive from him the strength to witness because if 'no one can say "Jesus is Lord" except by the Holy Spirit'

(1 Cor. 12:3), then who could give their life for Jesus if not under the action of the same Holy Spirit" (Cyril of Jerusalem, *Catecheses*, XVI, 21). For Tertullian the spirit is the "trainer" of the martyrs. He introduces them into the arena well prepared to face the fight and win: "You are about to face quite a fight, where the spectators and judges are God alone. The Holy Spirit is our trainer. The prize, an eternal crown. Our manager Jesus Christ, who has anointed you with the Holy Spirit and who has made you descend into the arena for the day of the fight, has taken you from the world of a comfortable life for a tough apprenticeship in order to train you more tenaciously" (*To the Martyrs*, III).

The magisterium of John Paul II follows this position when it insists on the contemporary need for the spirituality of martyrdom, recalling that the martyrs, in this century coming to an end, have adorned all of the Christian churches with their blood (see *UUS*, 84). "At the end of the second millennium, the Church has once again become a Church of martyrs....In our own century the martyrs have returned, many of them nameless, 'unknown soldiers' as it were of God's great cause" (*TMA*, 37). These martyrs, strengthened by the Spirit, become a sign of human freedom and dignity. "This revelation of freedom, and hence of man's true dignity, acquires a particular eloquence for Christians and for the Church in a state of persecution — both in ancient times and in the present — because the witnesses to divine truth then become a living proof of the action of the Spirit of truth present in the hearts and minds of the faithful, and they often mark with their own death by martyrdom the supreme glorification of human dignity" (*DeV*, 60).

All Christians are called to be witnesses to the Gospel with their own lives even if this does not necessarily require the martyrdom of blood but rather that of difficulties in life: loneliness, sickness, old age, poverty, being misunderstood, failure in life. In all these things the Spirit intervenes to make us experience, in trial and abandonment, "nothing but joy" (see James 1:2), to the point of that blessedness spoken of in 1 Peter: "If you are reviled for the name of Christ, you are blessed, because the Spirit of glory, which is the Spirit of God, is resting on you" (1 Pet. 4:14). It is not surprising that St. Francis of Assisi regarded this to be a grace: "Above all the graces and gifts of the Holy Spirit, the one that Christ gives to his friends, is to conquer oneself and for love of Christ voluntarily to endure pain, injury, disgrace, and discomfort" (*Little Flowers*, VIII).

The Holy Spirit inspires and strengthens the "successors of the martyrs," those men and women consecrated in religious life. "The consecrated life, deeply rooted in the example and teaching of Christ the Lord, is a gift of God the Father to his Church through the Holy Spirit" (*VC*, 1). Because of this, religious in search of Christian authenticity are committed to be "bearers of the Spirit" in a special way (see *VC*, 6; 19).

In the Spirit, these two forms of witnessing to Christ become models for every Christian, showing to all that sincerity of Christian life and commitment to the Gospel imply an uncompromising radicalness. Believers, therefore, by the power of Baptism and Confirmation (the sacrament of witness par excellence), guided by the Spirit become witnesses of Christ in their daily life knowing that to be Christian means to be ready to die for Christ at any moment. In this way, martyrdom extends throughout life. The perfect Christian, writes Clement of Alexandria, "will give witness (*martyrēsei*) at night, and give witness during the day. In word, life, and conduct the Christian will give witness. In living together with the Lord he will remain his confidant and table companion according to the Spirit. The Christian will remain pure in the flesh, pure in heart, sanctified in the word. 'The world has been crucified to me [Christ],' says the Scripture, and he is crucified 'to the world' (Gal. 6:14). The Christian, carrying everywhere the cross of the Savior, follows in the footsteps of the Lord and becomes, like God, holy among the holy" (*Stromata*, II, 20).

John Paul II recalls that the "new martyrs" include the heroic witness of many Christian spouses. "It will be the task of the Apostolic See, in preparation for the year 2000, to update the martyrologies for the universal Church, paying careful attention to the holiness of those who in our time lived fully by the truth of Christ. In particular, there is need to foster the recognition of the heroic virtues of men and women who have lived their Christian vocation in marriage. Precisely because we are convinced of the abundant fruits of holiness in the married state, we need to find the most appropriate means for discerning them and proposing them for the whole Church as a model and encouragement for other Christian spouses" (*TMA*, 37).

The Spirit distributes to everyone in their various states of life his charisms and stimulates them to give witness to the variegated beauty of the Church. Cyril of Alexandria said to the catechumens: "O grandeur of the Holy Spirit, admirable, omnipotent lavisher of charisms! Think of those here seated, souls in which he is present and works. He is observing the dispositions of everyone, scrutinizing thoughts and consciences, words and works.... Throughout the world we can see bishops, priests, deacons, monks, virgins, and lay faithful. At the head of all these is the Spirit who presides and distributes to each one his or her charism. Throughout the world he gives one purity, another perpetual virginity, another the gift of mercy, to another love for the poor or the power to chase out demons. As a light makes everything bright with one beam of its rays, so does the Holy Spirit illuminate all those who have eyes to see" (*Catecheses*, XVI, 22).

Asceticism in the Spirit

The action of the Spirit in the Christian is not automatic. It is not a passive attitude that is required, but a collaborative one, eliminating, above all, everything that can impede the work of the Holy Spirit. Macarius of Egypt affirms that the human will is essential if God is to act in humanity. "Human will is, so to speak, an essential condition; if this will does not exist, God cannot do anything" (*Homilies,* XXXVII, 10). This cooperation of humanity with God, purifying the soul from the dregs of sin and passion which impede a person from reflecting the image of God, is called in Christian tradition "asceticism." St. Gregory of Nyssa writes: "Because of sin each person's spirit is a broken mirror which, rather than reflecting God, reflects the image of shapeless matter" (*On the Creation of Man,* XII). As a result, passions upset the primitive harmony existing in the human being who finds it easier and more immediate to "like" something ephemeral rather than the Creator, the false image instead of the prototype.

The Spirit intervenes to help people reconstruct in themselves the image of God, according to the beautiful writing of Basil, bishop of Ceasarea. He summarizes this action of the Spirit in souls and the results that follow: "As regards the intimate union of the Spirit with the soul, this does not consist in a physical closeness...but in the exclusion of passions. The soul is purified from the ugliness acquired through vices, reassumes the beauty of its nature, and reestablishes the true image of its pristine form through purity. The Paraclete approaches us in this. The Spirit, like the sun falling on the purest of eyes, will show us in himself the image of the invisible. In the blessed contemplation of the image, you shall see the ineffable beauty of the Archetype. Through the Spirit the heart is elevated, the poor are led by the hand,

and the proficient become perfect" (*On the Holy Spirit,* IX, 23).

The Struggle against the "Flesh" to Acquire the "Fruit" of the Spirit

This process of purification accomplished in the Spirit is called in Galatians 5:13 and Romans 8:1–12 "the struggle against the flesh." Although human beings have been redeemed and the Spirit is already given, there still remains inherent in every human being the sad possibility of again becoming *flesh,* that is, the human being in a natural state, decadent, unredeemed, at the mercy of egoism, which makes everything, in an idolatrous manner, revolve around oneself. The Holy Spirit helps the believer to be liberated from this radical negative force. The Spirit enables us to follow the fundamental law of life, which consists in opening ourselves to God and to our brothers and sisters, orienting our lives according to the criteria of love. "Called to freedom" (Gal. 5:13), Christians can remain in this glorious filial condition only thanks to the intervention of the Spirit, guarantor and active principle of one's freedom. This is the reason for St. Paul's exhortation to "live by the Spirit" and to be "led by the Spirit": "Live by the Spirit, I say, and do not gratify the desires of the flesh. For what the flesh desires is opposed to the Spirit, and what the Spirit desires is opposed to the flesh; for these are opposed to each other, to prevent you from doing what you want. But if you are led by the Spirit, you are not subject to the law" (Gal. 5:16–18). It is well-known that the opposition between flesh and the Spirit exists within every believer. Believers already are the children of God and have the Spirit, but nefarious and centrifugal possibilities persist in each believer. The works of the flesh are "fornication, impurity, licentiousness, idolatry, sorcery, enmities, strife, jealousy, anger, quarrels, dissensions, factions, envy, drunkenness, carousing, and things like these" (Gal. 5:19–21). They are capable of returning us to the former condition of slavery and can suffocate the beautiful work of the Spirit. Christian morality is not a morality of slavery. It does not consist in a list of ethical norms imposed from outside. Instead, Christian morality is a "co-natural" way of acting by a "spiritualized" human being, a believer who has become in the Spirit "another Christ," living according to the logic of a "new life in Christ" (see Eph. 4:17–33) and of the "same mind" as Christ (Phil. 2:5). Thus does the Spirit open people to the logic of the Sermon on the Mount and the Beatitudes. In this perspective it will be easy to serve God because "we are slaves not under the old written code but in the new life of the Spirit" (Rom. 7:6). When this comes to pass the *fruit of the Spirit* will be resplendent in the life of the authentic Christian. This is the essential and original fruit of the Christian *agape-love:* "God's love has been poured into our hearts through the Holy Spirit that has been given to us" (Rom. 5:5). The gift of the Spirit is the seed of a harmonious moral life which the Christian is invited to achieve, a life characterized as animated by the Spirit. The various manifestations marking the Christian life are no less than the radiating of the original and fundamental gift of charity. The *Catechism,* citing the Vulgate, explains and lists the fruits of the Spirit. "The fruits of the Spirit are perfections that the Holy Spirit forms in us as the first fruits of eternal glory. The tradition of the Church lists twelve of them: 'charity, joy, peace, patience, kindness, goodness, generosity, gentleness, faithfulness, modesty, self-control, chastity' (Gal. 5:22–23, Vulgate)" (CCC, 1832).

Another fruit of the Spirit is *freedom,* which flows directly from charity and from the fact of being children of the Son. "The more one has charity, the more one has freedom, because 'where the Spirit of the Lord is, there is freedom'

(2 Cor. 3:17). He who has perfect charity has freedom to the highest degree" (Thomas Aquinas, *In III Sent.* d. 29, q. un., a. 8; q. 1, 3a.c.). St. Paul says: "For you were called to freedom, brothers and sisters.... But if you are led by the Spirit, you are not subject to the law" (Gal. 5:13, 18). Christians are free because they follow "the law of the Spirit" (see Rom. 8:2), which leads him to flee evil because of love and not because of fear. Thomas Aquinas teaches: "This is exactly when the Holy Spirit works. He interiorly perfects our spirit, communicating to it a new dynamism so that it refrains from evil for love.... In this way it is free, not in the sense that it is not subject to the divine law; it is free because its interior dynamism makes it do what divine law prescribes" (*In 2 Cor. 3:17,* lect. 3).

Clearly none of this is a mechanical process. This is a goal to which the Spirit alone leads, and in the measure to which the Christian accepts and supports his action. This is why the fruits of the Spirit are spoken of as a path, which evokes the idea of maturation. Christian life will be nothing less than continual growth, an advancing in the direction of the Spirit and under the impulse of the Spirit. This implies paying attention, listening to the Spirit, and following him in obedience throughout a life shaped by the strength and style of the Spirit. "If we live in the Spirit, let us also be guided by the Spirit" (Gal. 5:25).

Repentance in the Spirit

In the Sequence for the feast of Pentecost, the Church prays to the Holy Spirit: "Without your strength, nothing is in man, nothing without blame. Wash what is dirty, bathe what is dry, heal what is bleeding. Bend what is rigid, heat what is cold, straighten what is bent."

Life in Christ, "walking in the Spirit," is not always crowned with success. Christians often experience defeat and sin. At that very moment the Spirit does not abandon believers but rather intervenes with sweetness to lift up those who have fallen and place them back on track, asking repentance and granting forgiveness of sins. This is a true consolation that Scripture and tradition attest to in abundance.

In the abuse of freedom, we personally encounter the monstrous possibility of substituting ourselves for God, building up our own image and denying our nature as created beings. At the base of this is the drama of sin and alienation. In response Christ offers his forgiveness as a condition for conversion and reintegration into the holiness of the body of the Church. This return to the Father's house (see Luke 15:11–32), or change of orientation, is due to the Holy Spirit, as on Pentecost, after the descent of the Spirit and Peter's speech, those present felt "cut" in their hearts and were converted. "Now when they heard this, they were cut to the heart and said to Peter and to the other apostles, 'Brothers, what should we do?' Peter said to them, 'Repent, and be baptized every one of you in the name of Jesus Christ so that your sins may be forgiven; and you will receive the gift of the Holy Spirit' "(Acts 2:37–38). In this case the Spirit is first experienced as the one who moves souls and orients them toward God and then as the "sweet guest of the soul."

In the letter to the Romans, the Spirit is present as the one who frees us "from the law of sin and of death" (Rom. 8:2) and makes the repentant Christian the property of Christ (see Rom. 8:9). Jesus himself, in the outpouring of the Holy Spirit to the apostles on Easter night, relates the forgiveness of sins *with the Spirit:* "Receive the Holy Spirit. If you forgive the sins of any, they are forgiven them; if you retain the sins of any, they are retained" (John 20:22–23). The Spirit not only moves Christians to repent, but has the power to give and renew divine life. He can forgive sins when repentance exists, especially in the sacrament of penance. This sacrament is not the result of a mechanism of absolution, but of a miracle of conversion which only the Spirit can accomplish and which can occur only insofar as the priest and the penitent are pervaded by the Spirit. The Spirit accomplishes all this, creating and bestowing the "new heart" and thus establishing a new condition in the love for God and the acceptance of his will.

The conviction that sins are forgiven by the work of the Holy Spirit is found in the Eastern and Western Fathers. St. Ambrose says: "Let us see if the Holy Spirit forgives sins. But this cannot be in doubt from the moment that the Lord said, 'Receive the Holy Spirit: to those whose sins he forgives, they will be forgiven.' Here we see it is the work of the Holy Spirit by which sins are forgiven! But human beings have their own ministry in forgiving sins. They do not have the right to a special power. They do not forgive sins in their own name but in the name of the Father, the Son, and the Holy Spirit" (*On the Holy Spirit,* III, 137).

Cyril of Jerusalem presents the action of the Spirit within the totality of Christian life as the one who forgives, aids, and protects the entire life of the person baptized. "If you believe, you obtain more than the forgiveness of sins. You are enabled to accomplish actions beyond those of human strength. You could be worthy of the charism of prophecy! You will receive as much grace as you can hold.... He will take care of you like a soldier. He will watch your coming and your going, and he will keep an eye on whoever sets a snare for you. He will give you every type of charism, unless you sadden him with sin. It has been written: 'Do not sadden the Holy Spirit of God, by whom you have been sealed for the day of redemption' " (*Catecheses,* XVII, 37).

Renewal in the Spirit

The newness produced by the Spirit in every baptized person is that of forming the People of God. By taking part in the richness and responsibility that baptismal consecration and the anointing of Confirmation entail, believers rediscover the charismatic dimension of the entire Christian community. The Spirit opens the heart in every believer to a multiplicity of gifts with a view to their use to the community (see *LG* 3, 4, 11, 12b, 30), thus demonstrating the variety of ministries and charisms within the Church. Through the power of the Spirit the charismatic richness of the holy People of God is expressed in all of its personal and communitarian forms (lay associations, movements, organizations, etc.). At the basis of this is the rediscovery of the baptismal vocation in the announcement of the Gospel and in an authentic life choice. The Spirit is the Lord and giver of life of the ecclesial community, and the task of the Church is to activate in history the encounter of God and humanity accomplished in the incarnation of the Son. Because of this we understand why we find within ecclesial life the origin and the meaning of the gifts of the Spirit. Theologian and cardinal Yves Congar writes: "If it is impossible to think of a living God, the God of the covenant, without a people and a Church, it is even less plausible to think of a Church with a symphony of different gifts, of coresponsibility, of exchanges and communion without seeing God, in his Spirit, as the one who puts us in mutual contact, communicates, and makes communicate" (*Esprit de l'homme, esprit de Dieu*).

Within the Church, the richness of the spiritual gifts is associated with the diversity of ministries, which is geared to achieving the growth of the community in the fullness of truth. This is the profound sense of the flowering of "ecclesial movements" which characterizes the contemporary Church. The history of the Church has seen its community animated by a great number of charismatic expressions. The fathers of monasticism and the founders of the various religious orders have made the mysterious action of the Spirit visible. In the Church today, we continue to witness the same unchanging actions, expressed in the "church movements," as *Christifideles Laici* declares:"Alongside the traditional forming of associations, and at times coming from their very roots, movements and new sodalities have sprouted, with a specific feature and purpose, so great is the richness and the versatility of resources that the Holy Spirit nourishes in the ecclesial community, and so great is the capacity of initiative and the generosity of our lay people" (*ChL*, 29).

These movements are characterized by a renewed openness to the person of the Spirit, giver of every gift, who can be found within the experience of the daily rediscovery of the centrality of the Word as the guide for life. At the basis of the innovative strength of these movements is the importance of communion in life, in which knowing each other and encountering each other by walking together is the most meaningful moment. These movements, aligning themselves with the Church's extraordinary vitality, constitute a sign, especially with regard to the urgency of living the radicalness of the Christian faith in the most concrete instances of existence. In this way, they give witness that the Gospel is not alien to this world. The Gospel, in fact, is the yeast, the condiment able to provide meaning through life choices marked by freedom in the Spirit and the reasonings of hope.

Such experiences are not immune to risks, like taking refuge in privacy, accenting only the subjective dimension of the faith, concentrating activities within the movement or association. On the other hand, the majority of these groups express the ecclesial dimension characterized by the inseparable link between communion and mission. Fundamental criteria inspiring a spiritual renewal which aims at the roots of our Church's being and of which "ecclesial movements" are an expression include the primacy of every

Christian's vocation to holiness; the responsibility to profess the Catholic faith; the witness of a steadfast and committed communion; conformity with and participation in the apostolic goal of the Church; and a commitment to a social presence in human society which, in light of Church social doctrine, is at the service of integral human dignity (see *ChL*, 30). John Paul II affirms: "The Church tries to become more consciously aware of the Spirit which works in it for the good of its communion and mission, through the sacramental, hierarchical, and charismatic gifts. One of the Spirit's gifts in our time is certainly the flourishing of ecclesial movements. Since the beginning of my pontificate they have continued to demonstrate reasons for hope for the Church and humanity. They are a sign of the freedom in organization, in which the one Church is fulfilled, and represent a trustworthy newness, which still needs to be adequately understood in all its positive effectiveness for the Kingdom of God at work today in history. Within the framework for celebrating the Great Jubilee, I count on the witness and cooperation of the movements. This is true above all in 1998, with its special emphasis on the Holy Spirit and his sanctifying presence within the community of the disciples of Christ. I am confident that these movements, in communion with their pastors,...want to carry to the heart of the Church their spiritual, educational, and missionary richness, which are a precious experience and proposal for Christian life" ("The Holy Father's Homily for the Vigil of Pentecost," May 25, 1996).

Conclusion

From what has been said, it is obvious that the Spirit is truly the heart of Christian life and its very breath, to the point that it is not a case of our being "devoted" to the Holy Spirit but one of simply living and breathing the Spirit. Throughout the year dedicated to reflection on the Holy Spirit, we must recover some fundamental values of Christian living as lived and preached in the light of the Spirit. It is impossible to insist too much on the fact that sanctifying grace is not a *routine thing,* but the very life of God united to the believer in the gift of the Spirit. In the presence of sanctifying grace sin emerges in all its drama as an assault on the "spiritual" integrity of human beings. Salvation is not the fruit of human conquest but the outcome of the intimate relationship with God inscribed in the experience of divine filiation. Letting oneself be guided by the Spirit means to accept the gift of redemption as a condition for living one's life in finitude and fragility, as a witness, in today's world to the new creation which is the work of God's love. This is the arena of responsibility in which all believers are invited to live in service of witness and charity. Believers are called to build new relationships with others and with all reality. In this way they achieve their identity characterized above all as an exhilarating journey toward the freedom of a true experience in the Spirit. It is freeing oneself to love.

A page of the apostolic letter *Dominum et Vivificantem* sheds light on this: "When, under the influence of the Paraclete, people discover this divine dimension of their being and life, both as individuals and as a community, they are able to free themselves from the various determinisms which derive mainly from the materialistic bases of thought, practice, and related modes of action. In our age these factors have succeeded in penetrating into man's inmost being, into that sanctuary of the conscience where the Holy Spirit continually radiates the light and strength of new life in the 'freedom of the children of God.' Man's growth in this life is hindered by the conditionings and pressures exerted upon him by dominating structures and mechanisms in the various spheres of society. It can be said that in many cases social factors, instead of fostering the development and expansion of the human spirit, ultimately deprive the human spirit of the genuine truth of its being and life—over which the Holy Spirit keeps vigil—in order to subject it to the 'prince of this world.'

"The Great Jubilee of the year 2000 thus contains a message of liberation by the power of the Spirit, who alone can help individuals and communities to free themselves from the old and new determinisms by guiding them with the 'law of the Spirit, which gives life in Christ Jesus,' and thereby discovering and accomplishing the full measure of man's true freedom. For, as St. Paul writes, 'where the Spirit of the Lord is, there is freedom.' This revelation of freedom and hence of man's true dignity, acquires a particular eloquence for Christians and for the Church in a state of persecution — both in ancient times and the present — because the witnesses to divine truth then become a living proof of the action of the Spirit of truth present in the hearts and minds of the faithful, and they often mark with their own death by martyrdom the supreme glory of human dignity.

"Also in the ordinary conditions of society, Christians, as witnesses to man's authentic dignity, by their obedience to the Holy Spirit contribute to the manifold 'renewal of the face of the earth,' working together with their brothers and sisters in order to achieve and put to good use everything that is good, noble, and beautiful in the modern progress of civilization, culture, science, technology, and other areas of thought and human activity" (*DeV*, 60).

Rediscovering the importance of life in the Spirit will mean to reinforce the history of the fruitfulness of the Gospel and the effectiveness of its message. "For 'renewal in the Spirit' will be authentic and will have real fruitfulness in the Church, not so much according to how it gives rise to extraordinary charisms, but according to how it leads the greatest possible number of the faithful, as they travel their daily paths, to make a humble, patient, and persevering effort to know the mystery of Christ better and better, and to bear witness to it" (*CT,* 72).

Turning to the Spirit, then, means to invoke the gift of receptiveness to his actions. For this, we suggest a few prayers which, together with the well-known "Veni Creator" and the Sequence for Pentecost, the "Veni Sancte Spiritus" of the Latin rite, all the faithful can use to turn to the Spirit, especially before prayer or the reading the Word of God. This practice will place the lives of the faithful under the constant vivifying and healing action of the Paraclete.

"Heavenly Sovereign, Paraclete, Spirit of truth who are present everywhere and who fill all, treasure chest of every good and giver of life, come, live in us, cleanse us of every stain and, you who are good, save our souls. Amen." (Byzantine liturgy, Troparion of the Pentecost Vespers)

"Lord, grant to us the gifts of the Holy Spirit, and render us worthy to approach the holy of holies with pure heart and with irreproachable consciences." (*Anaphora of the Twelve Apostles*)

"O Holy Spirit, true God, you who like a marvelous, life-giving fire descended upon the apostles in the Upper Room, bestow the gifts of your wisdom on us." (Armenian liturgy)

"I ask you, O Father, to send your Holy Spirit into our souls and to make us understand the Scriptures inspired by him. May we interpret them in a pure and worthy

way so that all the faithful gathered here may profit."
(Serapion, *Euchologion,* 1)

"Come, true light. Come, eternal life. Come, hidden mystery. Come, treasure without name. Come, ineffable reality. Come, inconceivable person. Come, happiness without end. Come, light without sunset. Come, infallible hope of all who must be saved. Come, awakener of all who sleep. Come, resurrection of the dead. Come, O powerful one who ever make and remake everything and transform everything with your power alone. Come, O invisible one, totally intangible and impalpable. Come, you who always remain still and at the same time are constantly moving. Come to us who languish in the nether regions, you who are above all the heavens. Come, O beloved Name, everywhere invoked, whose being it is absolutely impossible for us to express, whose nature we can never know. Come, eternal joy. Come, incorruptible crown. Come, O scarlet robe of the great King, our God. Come, crystalline belt clustered with jewels. Come inaccessible sandal. Come, royal purple. Come, truly sovereign right hand. Come, you whom my miserable soul has always desired. Come, the Alone to the alone, for you see that I am alone. Come, you who have separated me from everything and made me a solitary person in this world. Come, you who have become your desire itself in me, you who have caused me to want you, you, the absolutely inaccessible. Come, my breath and my life. Come, consolation of my poor soul. Come, my joy, my glory, my delight for ever."
(Simeon the New Theologian, *Hymns,* 949–1022)

"Come, O come, most excellent counsellor of the suffering soul.... Come, you who cleanse from ugliness, you who cure plagues. Come, strength of the weak, supporter of the fallen. Come, doctor of the humble, conqueror of the proud. Come, O tender father of the orphans.... Come, hope of the poor.... Come, star of sailors, port of the shipwrecked. Come, O shining glory of all the living.... Come, you who are the holiest of the Spirits. Come and take pity on me. Conform me to yourself." (John of Fécamp, A.D. 1060)

Chapter 9

The Bride and the Spirit Say: Come

As we prepare to cross the threshold into the "Third Millennium," the memories of a millennium filled with unimaginable tragedies are still alive. The last world war alone counted sixty million deaths. Even today, threatening wars explode everywhere. It is said that the future will be composed of local wars. Today, in an era of high technology, millions of people, especially children, die of hunger and privation. If we do not feel the anxiety which characterized certain circles on the eve of the second millennium, it is because humans today are capable of lulling their fears to sleep. Although we live in a society containing all the elements to diminish hope, Christians are aware that there are solid reasons for hope.

Fundamental to Christian hope is the witness of resurrected life. In Christ, under the breath of the Spirit, Christians find a place of non-death. They discover within the innermost part of themselves that Someone who intervenes forever between them and nothing: the risen Christ, victor over death and hell. Christians can, therefore, dare to have the courage to love, the joy to live, because eternal life begins here and now. Taken comprehensively, Christian anthropology extends from Eden to the fullness of the Kingdom, embracing the mystery of beginning and ultimate end, even to the total salvation of humanity. In this sense the mystery of humanity is illuminated not only thanks to creation "in Christ," but also by means of that tension that cuts across all human existence and leads people "toward Christ." In the eschaton, human beings will not only be saved, but will also be fully integrated into communion with God. The maturation of history and its tension regarding the future has always been linked to the Spirit, who, with his coming, brings to completion the "last days" (see Acts 2:17).

The Spirit, Guarantee of the Resurrection

"Sent by the Father who hears the *epiclesis* of the Church, the Spirit gives life to those who accept him and is, even now, the 'guarantee' of their inheritance (Eph. 1:14; 2 Cor. 1:22)" (CCC, 1107). St. Paul said that the seal of the Lord is the seal with which the Holy Spirit marked believers "for the day of redemption" (Eph. 4:30) because "the Spirit is life because of righteousness. If the Spirit of him who raised Jesus from the dead dwells in you, he who raised Christ from the dead will give life to your mortal bodies also through his Spirit that dwells in you" (Rom. 8:10–11). For St. John, this life is already in our possession: "Whoever believes has eternal life" (John 6:47), since Christ himself dwells in the believer. "God has given us eternal life, and this life is his Son. Whoever has the Son has life" (1 John 5:11–12). The result is that we possess the Son through the Spirit who is life and gives life.

St. Paul affirms that the beginning of this life is already present in believers insofar as in the biblical perspective the truth of something is determined by its end, that is, that toward which one is moving. Christians possess the pledge of the Spirit. You "were marked with the seal of the promised Holy Spirit; this is the pledge of our inheritance toward redemption as God's own people, to the praise of his glory" (Eph. 1:13–14). St. Paul also says: "But it is God who establishes us with you in Christ and has anointed us, by putting his seal on us and giving us his Spirit in our hearts as a first installment" (2 Cor. 1:21–22). Now we have only the beginnings of life and because of this we are still "groaning" as in giving birth. But these are pains leading to definitive life.

Expectation and Judgment in the Spirit

In the various liturgies of the Church eschatological expectation is very intense. For example, in the Latin rite liturgy, after the consecration, we acclaim: "We proclaim your death, Lord Jesus, until you come in glory." The prayer following the Our Father, says: "Keep us free from sin and protect us from all anxiety as we wait in joyful hope for the coming of our Savior, Jesus Christ." This eschatological tension expressed in the liturgy is due to the "pledge" of the Spirit received by the Church. According to Preface VI of ordinary time: "We possess even now the first fruits of your Spirit, in whom you have raised Jesus Christ from the dead, and we live in the expectation that the blessed hope in the eternal Easter of your kingdom be fulfilled."

St. Basil says that the Holy Spirit not only drives the Christian toward expectation, but adds that at the end of time the seal imprinted on the redeemed will be the sign of final salvation. "If we reflect carefully, we will understand that even at the moment of the expected manifestation of the Lord from heaven, the Holy Spirit will not fail us as some believe. Instead, the Spirit will be present even on the day of the judgment of the Lord, when the Lord will judge the world in righteousness, he the blessed and only sovereign.... Those who have been marked with the seal of the Holy Spirit for the day of redemption and have preserved intact and not diminished the first fruits of the Spirit they have received will hear said to them: 'Well done, good and trustworthy slave; you have been trustworthy in a few things, I will put you in charge of many things' (Matt. 25:21)" (*On the Holy Spirit,* XVI, 40).

In the Parousia the judgment will be not only public but also an act that involves the intimacy of the human person. It will be a judgment that will come about with the intervention of the Spirit who is, at the same time, truth and love, by whom we will see ourselves in the light of that Truth and Love which is God. We will be able to judge ourselves without any masks and authentically, letting ourselves be pierced only by the sword of the Spirit and by the strength of the Word of God. Everyone "will be saved, but only as through a fire" (1 Cor. 3:15), a flame which consumes everything that is impure and inadequate for the Kingdom. To be forgiven it is necessary that every evil, all expressions of hate and self-centeredness that have settled in the human heart be eliminated through suffering and restitution be made thereby. This fire which burns and purifies is identified in ancient tradition with the Spirit. The so-called purification of "purgatory" is the love of the Spirit who, like a sword, pierces to the marrow of the bones.

"The earthly trajectory of life" says John Paul II, "has an end which, if reached in friendship with God, coincides with the first instant of the blessed life. Even if the soul in its passage to heaven is purified of its last dregs in purgatory, this soul is already filled with light, certainty, and joy because it knows that it belongs to God forever. At that culminating point the soul is guided to the Holy Spirit, author and giver not only of the justifying 'first grace' and of sanctifying grace throughout earthly life, but also of glorifying grace *in hora mortis*. It is the grace of final perseverance" (*EH*, 5).

The Ultimate Reality Begins Now in the Spirit

Humanity is already living the ultimate reality because the resurrection has broken into the world, transfiguring it into definitive salvation. At every moment the Parousia spreads its transfiguring light. The outpouring of the Spirit is already the beginning of the ultimate reality. "For those who possess the faith of the Word of God echoed in Christ and preached by the apostles, eschatology already has begun. It can even be said that it already is fulfilled in its fundamental aspect: the presence of the Holy Spirit in human history, which from Pentecost takes its meaning and vital impulse in the divine goal of every person and humanity as a whole. In the Old Testament the basis of hope was the promise of the perennial presence and providence of God, which would be manifested in the messiah. Hope in the New Testament, by the grace of the Holy Spirit who is at its origin, already has an anticipatory possession of future glory" (*EH*, 2).

The sacramental sign of the ultimate reality has already begun in the Spirit and is represented in the Eucharist, where the Spirit, through the *epiclesis,* descends from heaven and transforms tangible reality into a new creature, a new heaven and a new earth. The risen Christ is already present in the Eucharist. In him, humanity and the entire universe become a new creation. We taste the ultimate reality in the Eucharist. The world begins to become transformed and the Church be the community of *marana'tha.*

"One could say that Christian life on earth is like an initiation into full participation in the glory of God. And it is the Holy Spirit who constitutes the guarantee for achieving the fullness of eternal life, when by the effect of the redemption like pain and death, the rest of sins will be overcome" (*EH*, 2).

In Watchful Expectation

St. Paul teaches that the divine guarantee of the fulfillment of salvation is based on the gift of the Spirit. "And hope does not disappoint us, because God's love has been poured into our hearts through the Holy Spirit that has been given to us" (Rom. 5:5). To the question, "Who will separate us from the love of Christ?" (Rom. 8:35), the answer is decisive: nothing "will be able to separate us from the love of God in Christ Jesus our Lord" (Rom. 8:39). The desire of the apostle is that believers have an abundance of "hope by the power of the Holy Spirit" (Rom. 15:13). This is the basis of Christian optimism regarding the destiny of the world and the possibility of human salvation in all times, even the most difficult, on the path of history toward the perfect glorification of Christ — "He will glorify me" (John 16:14) — and believers' full participation in the history and in the glory of the Son of God.

The Second Vatican Council summarizes in a very beautiful way the cooperation and constant expectation of humanity on the road toward the day of final redemption: "So it is, united with Christ in the Church and marked with the Holy Spirit 'who is the guarantee of our inheritance' (Eph. 1:14) that we are truly called and indeed are children of God (see 1 John 3:1) though we have not yet appeared with Christ in glory (see Col. 3:4) in which we will be like to God, for we will see him as he is (see 1 John 3:2). 'While we are at home in the body we are away from the Lord' (2 Cor. 5:6) and having the first fruits of the Spirit we groan inwardly (see Rom. 8:23) and we desire to be with Christ (see Phil. 1:23). That same charity urges us to live more for him who died for us, and who rose again (see 2 Cor. 5:15). We make it our aim, then, to please the Lord in all things (see 2 Cor. 5:9) and we put on the armor of God that we may be able to stand against the wiles of the devil and resist in the evil day (see Eph. 6:11–13). Since we know neither the day nor the hour, we should follow the advice of the Lord and watch constantly so that, when the single course of our earthly life is completed (see Heb. 9:27), we may merit to enter with him into the marriage feast and be numbered among the blessed (see Matt. 25:31–46) and not, like the wicked and slothful servants (see Matt. 25:26), be ordered to depart into the eternal fire (see Matt. 25:41), into the outer darkness where 'men will weep and gnash their teeth' (Matt. 22:13; 25:30). Before we reign with Christ in glory we must all appear 'before the judgment seat of Christ, so that each one may receive good or evil, according to what he has done in the body' (2 Cor. 5:10), and at the end of the world 'they will come forth, those who have done good, to the resurrection of life, and those who have done evil, to the resurrection of judgment' (John 5:29; see Matt. 25:46). We reckon then that 'the sufferings of this present time are not worth comparing with the glory that is to be revealed to us (Rom. 8:18; see 2 Tim. 2:11–12), and strong in faith we look for 'the blessed hope, the appearing of the glory of our great God and Savior Jesus Christ (Titus 2:13) 'who will change our lowly body to be like his glorious body' (Phil. 3:21) and who will come 'to be glorified in his saints, and to be marvelled in all who have believed' (2 Thess. 1:10)" (*LG*, 48).

Crossing the Threshold of Hope

St. Hilary holds that the Holy Spirit is "the gift which bestows perfect hope" (*On the Trinity*, II, 1). Hope has become one of John Paul II's favorite themes. "Be not afraid!" he insists in his teaching, explaining in a speech the significance of hope and its role for Christians. "St. Paul tells the Corinthians that among the greatest permanent gifts, there is *hope* (see 1 Cor. 12:31). Hope has a fundamental role in Christian life, as has faith and love, although 'the greatest of these is love' (1 Cor. 13:13). Clearly, hope is not understood in a restrictive sense of a special and extraordinary gift, given to some for the benefit of the community. Instead, it is *a gift of*

the Holy Spirit offered to every person who in faith opens
to Christ. Pay special attention to this gift, especially in our
time, during which many humans — even many Christians —
debate among themselves about the illusions and myths of an
infinite capacity for self-redemption and self-fulfillment and
the temptation to pessimism in the expectation of frequent
disillusions and defeats" (*EH,* 1).

With hope the Christian is able to enter "the inner shrine
behind the curtain" (Heb. 6:19). "For the Spirit is given to
the Church in order that through his power the whole community of the people of God, however widely scattered and
diverse, may persevere in hope: that hope in which 'we have
been saved' (Rom. 8:24). It is the eschatological hope, the
hope of definitive fulfillment in God, the hope of the eternal
kingdom, that is brought about by participation in the life
of the Trinity. The Holy Spirit, given to the apostles as the
Counselor, *is the guardian and animator of this hope in the
heart of the Church*" (*DeV,* 66). The Spirit is the dynamic
force that inspires the lifestyle of Christians. "Hence it will
be important to gain a renewed appreciation of the Spirit as
the one who builds the kingdom of God within the course
of history and prepares its full manifestation in Jesus Christ,
stirring people's hearts and quickening in our world the seeds
of the full salvation which will come at the end of time.

"In this eschatological perspective, believers should be
called to a renewed appreciation of the theological virtue
of hope, which they have already heard proclaimed 'in the
word of the truth, the Gospel' (Col. 1:5). The basic attitude
of hope, on the one hand, encourages the Christian not to
lose sight of the final goal which gives meaning and value to
life, and on the other offers solid and profound reasons for
a daily commitment to transform reality in order to make it
correspond to God's plan.

"As the apostle Paul reminds us: 'We know that the whole

creation has been groaning in travail together until now; and not only the creation, but we ourselves, who have the first fruits of the Spirit, groan inwardly as we wait for adoption as sons, the redemption of our bodies. For in this hope we were saved' (Rom. 8:22–24). Christians are called to prepare for the Great Jubilee of the beginning of the Third Millennium by renewing their hope in the definitive coming of the kingdom of God, preparing for it daily in their hearts, in the Christian community to which they belong, in their particular social context, and in world history itself.

"There is also need for a better appreciation and understanding of the signs of hope present in the last part of this century, even though they often remain hidden from our eyes. In society in general, such signs of hope include: scientific, technological, and especially medical progress in the service of human life, a greater awareness of our responsibility for the environment, efforts to restore peace and justice wherever they have been violated, a desire for reconciliation and solidarity among different peoples, particularly in the complex relationship between the North and the South of the world. In the Church they include a greater attention to the voice of the Spirit through the acceptance of charisms and the promotion of the laity, a deeper commitment to the cause of Christian unity, and the increasing interest in dialogue with other religions and with contemporary culture" (*TMA*, 45–46).

In conclusion, it seems ever clearer that the spirituality of the Third Millennium cannot be a spirituality enclosed in itself or one which denies the world to come. It must be one of full transfiguration because it is filled with the Spirit of life and hope. It will be a spirituality of resurrection. "In the time leading up to the Third Millennium after Christ, while 'the Spirit and the bride say to the Lord Jesus: Come!' (Rev. 22:17) this prayer of theirs is filled, as always, with

the eschatological significance which is destined to give fullness of meaning to the celebration of the Great Jubilee. It is
a prayer concerned with the salvific destinies toward which
the Holy Spirit by his action opens hearts throughout the
history of man on earth. But at the same time this prayer
is directed toward a precise moment in history which high-
lights the 'fullness of time' marked by the year 2000. The
Church wishes to prepare for this Jubilee in the Holy Spirit,
just as the Virgin of Nazareth in whom the Word was made
flesh was prepared by the Holy Spirit" (*DeV,* 66).

   In the fullness of joy and Christian hope, the entire Church
and all of humanity unceasingly invoke the renewed outpouring of the Spirit on the New Millennium that is at the
gates, as acclaimed by the words of the Sequence for Pentecost: "Come, Holy Spirit, send us from heaven a ray of
your light. Come, father of the poor, come, giver of gifts,
come, light of our hearts. Perfect comforter, sweet guest of
the soul, sweetest relief."